Christina Latham-Koenig
Clive Oxenden
Paul Seligson

ENGLISH FILE
Elementary English-French Wordlist

Great Clarendon Street, Oxford, OX2 6DP, United Kingdom

Oxford University Press is a department of the University of Oxford.
It furthers the University's objective of excellence in research, scholarship,
and education by publishing worldwide. Oxford is a registered trade
mark of Oxford University Press in the UK and in certain other countries

© Oxford University Press 2012

The moral rights of the author have been asserted

First published in 2012

2017
10 9 8

No unauthorized photocopying

All rights reserved. No part of this publication may be reproduced, stored
in a retrieval system, or transmitted, in any form or by any means, without
the prior permission in writing of Oxford University Press, or as expressly
permitted by law, by licence or under terms agreed with the appropriate
reprographics rights organization. Enquiries concerning reproduction outside
the scope of the above should be sent to the ELT Rights Department, Oxford
University Press, at the address above

You must not circulate this work in any other form and you must impose
this same condition on any acquirer

Links to third party websites are provided by Oxford in good faith and for
information only. Oxford disclaims any responsibility for the materials
contained in any third party website referenced in this work

ISBN: 978 0 19 459834 7

Printed in China

This book is printed on paper from certified and well-managed sources

Elementary English–French Wordlist

File 1

Vocabulary Banks

DAYS AND NUMBERS

Monday n	/ˈmʌndeɪ/	Your first class is on _____.	lundi
Tuesday n	/ˈtjuːzdeɪ/	So Anna, your classes are on _____ mornings.	mardi
Wednesday n	/ˈwenzdeɪ/	I work on _____ mornings.	mercredi
Thursday n	/ˈθɜːzdeɪ/	The movie is on _____.	jeudi
Friday n	/ˈfraɪdeɪ/	Your last class is on _____.	vendredi
Saturday n	/ˈsætədeɪ/	See you on _____.	samedi
Sunday n	/ˈsʌndeɪ/	The shop is closed on _____.	dimanche
zero	/ˈzɪərəʊ/	The country code is ____ four four.	zéro
one	/wʌn/	I have ____ sister and two brothers.	un/une
two	/tuː/	I'll have a pizza and ____ colas, please.	deux
three	/θriː/	Can you name ____ countries in English?	trois
four	/fɔː/	I have a reservation for ____ nights.	quatre
five	/faɪv/	I have a reservation for ____ people.	cinq
six	/sɪks/	The shop is open ____ days a week.	six
seven	/ˈsevn/	I work _____ days a week.	sept
eight	/eɪt/	I have _____ aunts and uncles.	huit
nine	/naɪn/	It costs ____ pounds.	neuf
ten	/ten/	There are ____ girls in my class.	dix
eleven	/ɪˈlevn/	There are _____ boys in my class.	onze
twelve	/twelv/	I have _____ hours of English a week.	douze
thirteen	/θɜːˈtiːn/	It's _____ minutes past twelve.	treize
fourteen	/fɔːˈtiːn/	There are _____ computers in the class.	quatorze
fifteen	/fɪfˈtiːn/	The building has got _____ windows.	quinze
sixteen	/sɪksˈtiːn/	I live at number _____.	seize
seventeen	/sevnˈtiːn/	I am _____ and start my first job on Monday.	dix-sept
eighteen	/eɪˈtiːn/	I'm _____ years old and I'm a student.	dix-huit
nineteen	/naɪnˈtiːn/	Room _____ is on the first floor.	dix-neuf
twenty	/ˈtwenti/	There are _____ people in my class.	vingt
twenty-one	/twenti ˈwʌn/	My sister is _____ years old.	vingt et un
thirty	/ˈθɜːti/	The train leaves at five _____.	trente

thirty-five	/ˈθɜːti ˈfaɪv/	My aunt is _____ years old.	trente-cinq
forty	/ˈfɔːti/	My dad is _____ years old.	quarante
forty-three	/fɔːti ˈθriː/	My mum is _____ years old.	quarante-trois
fifty	/ˈfɪfti/	It costs ____ cents.	cinquante
fifty-nine	/fɪfti ˈnaɪn/	Room _____ is on the second floor.	cinquante-neuf
sixty	/ˈsɪksti/	Passengers on flight BA234 please go to gate ____ immediately.	soixante
sixty-seven	/sɪksti ˈsevn/	My grandmother is _____ years old.	soixante-sept
seventy	/ˈsevnti/	My grandfather is _____ years old.	soixante-dix, septante [Belgique, Suisse]
seventy-two	/sevnti ˈtuː/	The British Airways flight to Madrid is boarding at gate _____.	soixante-douze, septante-deux [Belgique, Suisse]
eighty	/ˈeɪti/	The address is _____ Park Road.	quatre-vingts, huitante [Suisse]
eighty-eight	/eɪti ˈeɪt/	Open your books to page _____.	quatre-vingt-huit, huitante-huit [Suisse]
ninety	/ˈnaɪnti/	It's about _____ kilometres to Bordeaux.	quatre-vingt-dix, nonante [Belgique, Suisse]
ninety-four	/naɪnti ˈfɔː/	Take bus number _____.	quatre-vingt-quatorze, nonante-quatre [Belgique, Suisse]
a/one hundred	/ə/wʌn ˈhʌndrəd/	Open your books to page _____.	cent

THE WORLD

Africa n	/ˈæfrɪkə/	Egypt is in _____.	Afrique
African adj	/ˈæfrɪkən/	I am _____. I come from Nigeria.	africain(e)
American adj	/əˈmerɪkən/	Are you _____?	américain(e)
Argentina n	/ɑːdʒənˈtiːnə/	_____ is in South America.	Argentine
Argentinian adj	/ɑːdʒənˈtɪniən/	My friend is _____.	argentin(e)
Asia n	/ˈeɪʒə/	Japan is in ____.	Asie
Asian adj	/ˈeɪʒn/	I like _____ food.	asiatique
Australia n	/ɒˈstreɪliə/	Canberra is the capital of _____.	Australie
Australian adj	/ɒˈstreɪliən/	I'm not English. I'm _____.	australien(ne)
Brazil n	/brəˈzɪl/	I live in Rio de Janeiro, in _____.	Brésil
Brazilian adj	/brəˈzɪliən/	The teacher is _____.	brésilien(ne)
China n	/ˈtʃaɪnə/	She's from _____.	Chine
Chinese adj	/tʃaɪˈniːz/	My teacher is _____.	chinois(e)
Czech adj	/tʃek/	I am _____.	tchèque
the Czech Republic n	/tʃek rɪˈpʌblɪk/	I am from _____.	République tchèque
Egypt n	/ˈiːdʒɪpt/	_____ is in North Africa.	Égypte
Egyptian adj	/iˈdʒɪpʃn/	There are lots of _____ people in my class.	égyptien(ne)
England n	/ˈɪŋglənd/	London is the capital of _____.	Angleterre
English adj	/ˈɪŋglɪʃ/	Are you _____?	anglais(e)
Europe n	/ˈjʊərəp/	Italy is in _____.	Europe
European adj	/jʊərəˈpiːən/	Britain is part of the _____ Union.	européen(ne)
France n	/frɑːns/	_____ is next to Belgium.	France
French adj	/frentʃ/	My mother is _____.	français(e)

English	IPA	Example	French
German *adj*	/ˈdʒɜːmən/	The waitress is _____.	allemand(e)
Germany *n*	/ˈdʒɜːməni/	_____ is in Europe.	Allemagne
Hungarian *adj*	/hʌŋˈɡeəriən/	Frida is from Budapest – she's _____.	hongrois(e)
Hungary *n*	/ˈhʌŋɡəri/	_____ is near Austria.	Hongrie
Ireland *n*	/ˈaɪələnd/	I am from _____.	Irlande
Irish *adj*	/ˈaɪrɪʃ/	Dublin is an _____ city.	irlandais(e)
Italian *adj*	/ɪˈtæliən/	That actress is _____.	italien(ne)
Italy *n*	/ˈɪtəli/	I think Lake Garda is in ____.	Italie
Japan *n*	/dʒəˈpæn/	I think Kyoto is in _____.	Japon
Japanese *adj*	/dʒæpəˈniːz/	They are _____.	japonais(e)
Mexican *adj*	/ˈmeksɪkən/	_____ food is my favourite.	mexicain(e)
Mexico *n*	/ˈmeksɪkəʊ/	_____ is south of the USA.	Mexique
North America *n*	/nɔːθ əˈmerɪkə/	Canada is in _____.	Amérique du Nord
North American *adj*	/nɔːθ əˈmerɪkən/	The USA is a _____ country.	nord-américain(e)
Poland *n*	/ˈpəʊlənd/	She is from _____	Pologne
Polish *adj*	/ˈpəʊlɪʃ/	She is _____.	polonais(e)
Russia *n*	/ˈrʌʃə/	Moscow is the capital of _____.	Russie
Russian *adj*	/ˈrʌʃn/	I think it's _____, but I'm not sure.	russe
Scotland *n*	/ˈskɒtlənd/	Where are you from in _____?	Écosse
Scottish *adj*	/ˈskɒtɪʃ/	Are they _____?	écossais(es)
South America *n*	/saʊθ əˈmerɪkə/	Brazil is in _____.	Amérique du Sud
South American *adj*	/saʊθ əˈmerɪkən/	Argentina is a _____ country.	sud-américain(e)
Spain *n*	/speɪn/	Madrid is the capital of _____.	Espagne
Spanish *adj*	/ˈspænɪʃ/	I love _____ music.	espagnol(e)
Swiss *adj*	/swɪs/	I love _____ chocolate.	suisse
Switzerland *n*	/ˈswɪtsələnd/	I am going skiing in _____	Suisse
Turkey *n*	/ˈtɜːki/	Istanbul is in _____.	Turquie
Turkish *adj*	/ˈtɜːkɪʃ/	I love _____ food.	turc/turque
the (United) States/the US(A) *n*	/juːˌnaɪtɪd ˈsteɪts/	We're from Columbus, Ohio, in _____.	les États-Unis

CLASSROOM LANGUAGE

English	IPA	Example	French
Answer the questions.	/ˈɑːnsə ðə ˈkwestʃənz/	Read the text. _____	Répondez aux questions.
Can I have a copy, please?	/kæn aɪ həv ə ˈkɒpi pliːz/	_____ I haven't got one.	Puis-je avoir un exemplaire, s'il vous plaît ?
Can you help me, please?	/kæn ju ˈhelp mi pliːz/	_____ I have a problem.	Pouvez-vous m'aider, s'il vous plaît ?
Close the door.	/kləʊz ðə dɔː/	_____. It's cold outside.	Fermez la porte.
Do exercise a.	/du ˈeksəsaɪz eɪ/	_____ It's on the left.	Faites l'exercice a.
Excuse me, what's…in English?	/ɪkˈskjuːs mi wɒts…ɪn ˈɪŋɡlɪʃ/	_____ fromage _____	Excusez-moi, comment dit-on… en anglais ?
Go to page 84.	/ɡəʊ tə peɪdʒ ˈeɪti fɔː/	Open your books please. _____.	Allez à la page 84.
How do you spell it?	/haʊ də ju ˈspel ɪt/	_____ D-A-R-L-Y.	Comment ça s'écrit ?
I don't know.	/aɪ dəʊnt ˈnəʊ/	I'm sorry. _____	Je ne sais pas.

English	Pronunciation	Example	French
I don't understand.	/aɪ dəʊnt ˌʌndə'stænd/	_____ Can you repeat that, please?	Je ne comprends pas.
Listen and repeat.	/'lɪsn ən rɪ'piːt/	_____ Look at the words.	Écoutez et répétez.
Look at the board.	/lʊk ət ðə 'bɔːd/	_____ Repeat these sounds.	Regardez le tableau.
Open your books, please.	/'əʊpən jɔː bʊks pliːz/	OK, everyone. _____.	Ouvrez vos livres, s'il vous plaît.
Please stop talking!	/pliːz stɒp 'tɔːkɪŋ/	_____	Taisez-vous s'il vous plaît.
Read the text.	/riːd ðə 'tekst/	_____ Answer the questions.	Lisez le texte.
Sit down.	/sɪt 'daʊn/	_____ and open your books.	Asseyez-vous.
Sorry I'm late.	/'sɒri aɪm leɪt/	_____ There is a lot of traffic.	Désolé(e), je suis en retard.
Sorry, can you repeat that, please?	/'sɒri kæn ju rɪ'piːt ðæt pliːz/	I don't understand. _____	Excusez-moi, pouvez-vous répéter s'il vous plaît ?
Stand up.	/stænd 'ʌp/	_____ Speak to the other students.	Levez-vous.
Turn off your mobile.	/tɜːn ɒf jɔː 'məʊbaɪl/	_____ Please stop talking!	Éteignez votre téléphone portable, GSM [Belgique], natel [Suisse].
What page is it?	/wɒt 'peɪdʒ ɪz ɪt/	Sorry, I didn't hear you. _____	C'est à quelle page ?
Work in pairs/groups.	/wɜːk ɪn 'peəz/'gruːps/	_____ Practise the dialogue.	Travaillez en binômes/groupes.

Useful words and phrases

English	Pronunciation	Example	French
bike n	/baɪk/	I go to work by ____.	vélo
board n	/bɔːd/	Look at the ____.	tableau
cat n	/kæt/	I have a ____ at home.	chat
chair n	/tʃeə/	Take a seat on the ____.	chaise
computer n	/kəm'pjuːtə/	There is a ____ in the classroom.	ordinateur
desk n	/desk/	I write at a ____.	bureau
door n	/dɔː/	The ____ is at the front of the room.	porte
Good afternoon	/gʊd ˌɑːftə'nuːn/	_____, Sir.	Bonjour
Good evening	/gʊd 'iːvnɪŋ/	_____, Madam.	Bonsoir
Good morning	/gʊd 'mɔːnɪŋ/	_____, how are you?	Bonjour
Good night	/ˌgʊd'naɪt/	_____, see you in the morning.	Bonne nuit
I think it's…	/aɪ 'θɪŋk ɪts…/	_____ in Italy.	Je crois que c'est
I'm not sure	/aɪm nɒt 'ʃɔː/	I think it's Russian, but _____.	Je ne suis pas sûr(e)
name n	/neɪm/	My ____ is Paul.	nom
table n	/'teɪbl/	The teacher has a ____ at the front of the room.	table
thanks	/θæŋks/	_____ a lot.	merci
this det	/ðɪs/	____ is my first time in the UK.	ce, c'est
train n	/treɪn/	The ____ waiting at platform 13 is the Eurostar to Paris.	train
tree n	/triː/	There is a ____ in my garden.	arbre
weekday n	/'wiːkdeɪ/	Monday is a ____ in most countries.	jour de semaine
weekend n	/ˌwiː'kend/	The ____ is Saturday and Sunday in many countries.	week-end
well adj	/wel/	Very ____, thank you.	bien
window n	/'wɪndəʊ/	There is a ____ in our class.	fenêtre
Would you like…?	/wəd ju laɪk…/	_____ a coffee?	Voulez-vous…?

More words in File 1

address *n*	/əˈdres/	What's your _____?	adresse
age *n*	/eɪdʒ/	I won't tell you my ___.	âge
airport *n*	/ˈeəpɔːt/	People go to the _____ before and after a holiday.	aéroport
answer *v*	/ˈɑːnsə/	Read the text and _____ the questions.	répondre
bar *n*	/bɑː/	The _____ closes at 11.30 p.m.	bar
basketball *n*	/ˈbɑːskɪtbɔːl/	_____ is a popular American sport.	basketball
boot *n*	/buːt/	Where is my other ___?	botte
car *n*	/kɑː/	My ___ is old but fast.	voiture
chess *n*	/tʃes/	_____ is a slow game.	échecs
city *n*	/ˈsɪti/	Is it a ___ or a country?	ville
class *n*	/klɑːs/	Your first ___ is on Monday.	cours
country *n*	/ˈkʌntri/	What _____ is pizza from?	pays
double room *n*	/ˈdʌbl ruːm/	I'd like a _____ for two nights, please.	chambre double
email *n*	/ˈiːmeɪl/	What's you _____ address?	e-mail
first name *n*	/ˈfɜːst neɪm/	My _____ is Lisa.	prénom
ground floor *n*	/graʊnd flɔː/	Your room is on the _____.	rez-de-chaussée
hotel *n*	/həʊˈtel/	My ___ is near the museum.	hôtel
internet *n*	/ˈɪntənet/	I use the _____ every day.	internet
jazz *n*	/dʒæz/	I like ___ music.	jazz
lift *n*	/lɪft/	Take the ___ to the second floor.	ascenseur, lift [Suisse]
phone *n*	/fəʊn/	What's your _____ number?	téléphone
phone number *n*	/fəʊn ˈnʌmbə/	What's your _____?	numéro de téléphone
picture *n*	/ˈpɪktʃə/	Look at the _____ of a classroom.	photo
postcode *n*	/ˈpəʊstkəʊd/	My _____ is B4 6EU.	code postal
reception *n*	/rɪˈsepʃn/	Check in at _____.	réception
salad *n*	/ˈsæləd/	I like ___ with my pasta.	salade
school *n*	/skuːl/	_____ starts at 9.00 a.m.	école
single room *n*	/ˈsɪŋgl ruːm/	I'd like a _____, please.	chambre individuelle/simple
surname *n*	/ˈsɜːneɪm/	My _____ is Robertson.	nom de famille
taxi *n*	/ˈtæksi/	Take a ___ to the station.	taxi
tennis *n*	/ˈtenɪs/	I play ___ at the weekend.	tennis

File 2

Vocabulary Banks

THINGS

book *n*	/bʊk/	I am looking for a ___ to read.	livre
coin *n*	/kɔɪn/	There is a ___ on the table.	pièce

credit card n	/ˈkredɪt kɑːd/	I don't have a _____.	carte bancaire
diary n	/ˈdaɪəri/	I use a _____ at work.	agenda
dictionary n	/ˈdɪkʃənri/	Look up the word in a _____.	dictionnaire
file n	/faɪl/	I keep my work in a ___.	fichier
glasses pl n	/ˈɡlɑːsɪz/	He wears _____ to help him see.	lunettes
headphones pl n	/ˈhedfəʊnz/	He uses _____ to listen to music.	écouteurs
identity card n	/aɪˈdentəti kɑːd/	I have a passport, but I don't have an _____.	carte d'identité
iPod n	/ˈaɪpɒd/	I use an ____ to listen to music.	iPod
key n	/kiː/	Here is a ___ for your room.	clé
laptop n	/ˈlæptɒp/	I have a _____ for work.	ordinateur portable, portable [Suisse]
magazine n	/mæɡəˈziːn/	I buy a _____ every week.	magazine
mobile (phone) n	/ˈməʊbaɪl (fəʊn)/	I want a _____ for my birthday.	portable (téléphone), GSM [Belgique], natel [Suisse]
newspaper n	/ˈnjuːzpeɪpə/	I read a _____ every morning.	journal
pen n	/pen/	I use a ___ to write.	stylo
pencil n	/ˈpensl/	I use a _____ to write. It's easier to correct.	crayon
photo n	/ˈfəʊtəʊ/	There is a _____ of my family in my wallet.	photo
piece of paper n	/piːs əv ˈpeɪpə/	Can I have a _____ to write on?	feuille de papier
purse n	/pɜːs/	I keep my credit cards in a ____.	porte-monnaie
scissors pl n	/ˈsɪzəz/	I need some _____ to cut this paper.	ciseaux
stamp n	/stæmp/	I need a _____ to post this letter.	timbre
sunglasses pl n	/ˈsʌnɡlɑːsɪz/	It's really sunny. Where are my _____?	lunettes de soleil
ticket n	/ˈtɪkɪt/	A _____ to Oxford, please.	ticket, billet
tissue n	/ˈtɪʃuː/	Have you got a _____?	mouchoir en papier
umbrella n	/ʌmˈbrelə/	It's raining. I need to buy an _____.	parapluie
wallet n	/ˈwɒlɪt/	I keep my money in a _____.	portefeuille
watch n	/wɒtʃ/	What's this in English? ~ It's a _____.	montre

ADJECTIVES

attractive adj	/əˈtræktɪv/	He's quite tall and he's very _____.	attirant(e)
bad adj	/bæd/	This food is really ___.	mauvais(e)
beautiful adj	/ˈbjuːtɪfl/	She's a very _____ actress.	beau/belle
big adj	/bɪɡ/	His house is very ___. It's got six bedrooms.	grand(e)
blonde adj	/blɒnd/	He has got _____ hair.	blond(e)
cheap adj	/tʃiːp/	This restaurant is really _____.	bon marché
clean adj	/kliːn/	The window is really _____.	propre
cold adj	/kəʊld/	Are you hot, Suzy? ~ No, I'm ____.	froid(e)
dangerous adj	/ˈdeɪndʒərəs/	Careful! That dog's _____.	dangereux/dangereuse
dark adj	/dɑːk/	She has ____ hair.	brun(e)
difficult adj	/ˈdɪfɪkəlt/	This is a _____ exercise.	difficile
dirty adj	/ˈdɜːti/	My room is ____. I need to clean it.	sale
easy adj	/ˈiːzi/	The homework is ____.	facile

empty *adj*	/ˈempti/	Your glass is _____. Would you like another drink?	vide
expensive *adj*	/ɪkˈspensɪv/	That hotel is too _____. Let's book another one.	cher/chère
far *adj*	/fɑː/	It's not ___ now. Only 10 kilometres.	loin
fast *adj*	/fɑːst/	Her car is very ___.	rapide
fat *adj*	/fat/	My pet dog loves to eat and is very ___.	gros/grosse
full *adj*	/fʊl/	The hotel is ___.	complet/complète
good *adj*	/gʊd/	Don't worry. You know I'm a _____ driver.	bon/bonne
good-looking *adj*	/ˌgʊd ˈlʊkɪŋ/	He's a _____ man.	séduisant(e)
high *adj*	/haɪ/	Their house is ___ in the mountains.	haut(e), en altitude
hot *adj*	/hɒt/	The water is very ___.	chaud(e)
long *adj*	/lɒŋ/	He has ___ hair and brown eyes.	long/longue
low *adj*	/ləʊ/	The price is quite ___.	bas/basse
near *adj*	/nɪə/	I know another hotel ___ here.	près
new *adj*	/njuː/	This is a ___ jacket. My other one was too old.	neuf/neuve
old *adj*	/əʊld/	My car is really ___. I need a new one.	vieux/vieille
poor *adj*	/pɔː/	He is a ___ man. He doesn't have much money.	pauvre
pretty *adj*	/ˈprɪti/	She's tall and very _____.	joli(e)
quite *adv*	/kwaɪt/	It's ___ nice here.	plutôt, tout à fait
really *adv*	/ˈriːəli/	I _____ like Italian food.	vraiment
rich *adj*	/rɪtʃ/	Look at his clothes. He's very ___.	riche
right *adj*	/raɪt/	Well done, that's the _____ answer.	correct(e)
safe *adj*	/seɪf/	I am a ___ driver.	prudent(e)
short *adj*	/ʃɔːt/	She's quite _____ and slim.	petit(e)
slow *adj*	/sləʊ/	I don't like _____ service in a restaurant.	lent(e)
small *adj*	/smɔːl/	My bedroom is quite _____, but I love it.	petit(e)
strong *adj*	/strɒŋ/	My bag is heavy. I'm not _____ enough to lift it.	fort(e)
tall *adj*	/tɔːl/	He's quite ___ and he's very attractive.	grand(e)
thin *adj*	/θɪn/	Only ___ people can wear that.	mince
ugly *adj*	/ˈʌgli/	It's a really ___ picture.	laid(e)
very *adv*	/ˈveri/	It's ___ exciting!	très
weak *adj*	/wiːk/	He is too _____ to lift the bag.	faible
wrong *adj*	/rɒŋ/	Number five is the _____ answer.	incorrect(e)
young *adj*	/jʌŋ/	She's very _____. She's only five.	jeune

Useful words and phrases

angry *adj*	/ˈæŋgri/	I'm _____ with Dan.	furieux/furieuse, en colère
black *adj*	/blæk/	I wear _____ shoes to work.	noir(e)
blue *adj*	/bluː/	I like ___ jeans.	bleu
bored *adj*	/bɔːd/	I'm _____ with this homework.	lassé(e), fatigué(e)
brown *adj*	/braʊn/	He has black hair and _____ eyes.	marron
day *n*	/deɪ/	It's a lovely ___ today.	journée, jour

eyes pl n	/aɪz/	He has brown ____.	yeux
food n	/fuːd/	Harry loves all types of ____.	nourriture
green adj	/griːn/	My car is ____.	vert(e)
grey adj	/greɪ/	My grandmother's hair is ____.	gris(e)
hair n	/heə/	She has long brown ____.	cheveux
happy adj	/ˈhæpi/	I'm _____ you can come to the party.	heureux/heureuse
hungry adj	/ˈhʌŋgri/	I'm _____ – can I make a sandwich?	faim
lamp n	/læmp/	On my desk I have a computer and a ____.	lampe
mother n	/ˈmʌðə/	I live with my _____ and father.	mère
nice adj	/naɪs/	Have a ____ day!	bon/bonne
orange adj	/ˈɒrɪndʒ/	He has an _____ T-shirt.	orange
page n	/peɪdʒ/	Look at ____ 10, please.	page
pink adj	/pɪŋk/	My bedroom is ____.	rose
printer n	/ˈprɪntə/	I have a laptop and a _____ on my desk.	imprimante
red adj	/red/	She's got ____ hair.	roux/rousse
sad adj	/sæd/	Julie is ____ she can't come to the party.	triste
stressed adj	/strest/	I'm _____ – I need a holiday.	stressé(e)
that det	/ðæt/	Let's stop at ____ service station.	ce, cet, cette
these det	/ðiːz/	_____ are very difficult exercises.	ces
thing n	/θɪŋ/	What is that _____ there?	chose
thirsty adj	/ˈθɜːsti/	I'm _____ – where's the water?	assoiffé(e), avoir soif
those det	/ðəʊz/	What are ____ things there?	ces
thumb n	/θʌm/	My _____ on my right hand hurts.	pouce
tired adj	/ˈtaɪəd/	I'm ____ and I want to go to bed.	fatigué(e)
white adj	/waɪt/	I have a new _____ shirt.	blanc/blanche
worried adj	/ˈwʌrid/	I'm _____ about Gareth.	inquiet/inquiète
yellow adj	/ˈjeləʊ/	Taxis in New York are _____.	jaune

More words in File 2

about adv	/əˈbaʊt/	My teacher is _____ 40 years old.	environ
accent n	/ˈæksent/	She's from Glasgow, and she has a Scottish _____.	accent
actor/actress n	/ˈæktə/ˈæktrəs/	She's a French _____.	acteur/actrice
Be careful!	/bi ˈkeəfl/	_____ There's another car!	Sois/Soyez prudent !
Be quiet!	/bi ˈkwaɪət/	_____ I'm trying to read.	Tais-toi/Taisez-vous !
box n	/bɒks/	What is in that ____?	boîte
bull n	/bʊl/	That ____ is angry.	taureau
but conj	/bʌt/	She lives in Madrid, ____ she isn't Spanish.	mais
clock n	/klɒk/	I have a ____ in my kitchen.	pendule, horloge
Don't worry.	/dəʊnt ˈwʌri/	_____ I'm a good driver.	Ne t'inquiète/vous inquiétez pas.
famous adj	/ˈfeɪməs/	He's a _____ American actor.	célèbre
for example	/fɔː ɪgˈzɑːmpl/	Some words are British English, _____: mobile phone.	par exemple

horse n	/hɔːs/	My brother has a _____ called Bob.	cheval
jeans pl n	/dʒiːnz/	I wear _____ at the weekend.	jean
meaning n	/ˈmiːnɪŋ/	I don't understand the _____ of this word.	signification
money n	/ˈmʌni/	I keep my _____ in my wallet.	argent
politician n	/ˌpɒləˈtɪʃn/	My father is a _____.	homme politique
similar adj	/ˈsɪmələ/	American grammar is very _____ to British grammar.	similaire
singer n	/ˈsɪŋə/	Lady Gaga is a famous _____.	chanteur/chanteuse
Slow down!	/sləʊ ˈdaʊn/	_____	Ralentis/Ralentissez !
snake n	/sneɪk/	This _____ is brown and yellow.	serpent
sportsman/sportswoman n	/ˈspɔːtsmən/ˈspɔːtswʊmən/	Rafael Nadal is a famous _____.	sportif/sportive
story n	/ˈstɔːri/	Listen to the end of the _____.	histoire
Turn right.	/tɜːn ˈraɪt/	_____	Tourne/tournez à droite.
TV presenter n	/ˌtiː ˈviː prɪˈzentə/	My best friend is a _____ for the BBC.	présentateur/présentatrice télé
vice versa adv	/ˌvaɪs ˈvɜːsə/	You can travel from Delhi to Mumbai, and _____.	vice versa
What colour is...?	/wɒt ˈkʌlər ɪz.../	_____ the American flag?	De quelle couleur est... ?
zebra n	/ˈzebrə/	Look at that _____ over there.	zèbre

File 3

Vocabulary Banks

VERB PHRASES

cook v	/kʊk/	I _____ dinner for my family every evening.	cuisiner
drink v	/drɪŋk/	I _____ mineral water every day.	boire
eat v	/iːt/	I don't want to ___ fast food for dinner.	manger
go v	/gəʊ/	We __ to the cinema every month.	aller
have v	/hæv/	We don't _____ children but we have a dog.	avoir
like v	/laɪk/	I ___ animals so I have a cat, a dog, and a rabbit at home.	aimer
listen v	/ˈlɪsn/	I _____ to music on my iPod.	écouter
live v	/lɪv/	I ___ in a flat with my sister.	habiter
play v	/pleɪ/	You _____ tennis really well.	jouer
read v	/riːd/	I _____ a newspaper on the train every morning.	lire
say v	/seɪ/	You're late – ___ sorry to your teacher.	dire
speak v	/spiːk/	British and American people _____ the same language.	parler
study v	/ˈstʌdi/	I want to _____ economics at university.	étudier
take v	/teɪk/	I _____ an umbrella in my school bag every day.	prendre
want v	/wɒnt/	I _____ a new car – a BMW!	vouloir
watch v	/wɒtʃ/	I _____ TV on Saturday evenings.	regarder
wear v	/weə/	Do you _____ glasses for reading?	porter
work v	/wɜːk/	I _____ in an office in the town centre.	travailler

JOBS

administrator n	/əd'mɪnɪstreɪtə/	Karen is an _____.	administrateur/administratrice
architect n	/'ɑːkɪtekt/	Norman Foster is an _____.	architecte/architecte
bank manager n	/'bæŋk mænɪdʒə/	I want to be a _____ and make lots of money.	directeur/directrice de banque
builder n	/'bɪldə/	Carl is a _____ and he works very hard.	maçon
chef n	/ʃef/	Marco is a ____ in an Italian restaurant.	chef/chef cuisinier
cook n	/kʊk/	Julie is a _____ at the school.	cuisinier/cuisinière
dentist n	/'dentɪst/	I want to see a _____ about my bad teeth.	dentiste
doctor n	/'dɒktə/	I don't feel well. I need to see a _____.	docteur
engineer n	/endʒɪ'nɪə/	We need an _____ to help with this project.	ingénieur
factory worker n	/'fæktəri wɜːkə/	My uncle is a _____ _____ in a biscuit factory.	ouvrier/ouvrière
flight attendant n	/'flaɪt ətendənt/	She travels a lot. We think she's a _____.	steward/hôtesse de l'air
footballer n	/'fʊtbɔːlə/	My friend is a _____ He plays for Manchester United.	footballeur/footballeuse
hairdresser n	/'heədresə/	I'm a _____ I cut people's hair.	coiffeur/coiffeuse
journalist n	/'dʒɜːnəlɪst/	My dad is a _____. He writes for a newspaper.	journaliste
lawyer n	/'lɔːjə/	My mother is a _____.	avocat/avocate
model n	/'mɒdl/	Gisele Bundchen is a _____.	mannequin
musician n	/mjuː'zɪʃn/	My brother is a famous _____.	musicien
nurse n	/nɜːs/	A _____ usually works in a hospital.	infirmier/infirmière
pilot n	/'paɪlət/	A ____ flies planes.	pilote
policeman/policewoman n	/pə'liːsmən/pə'liːswʊmən/	There's a _____ outside our house.	policier/policière
receptionist n	/rɪ'sepʃənɪst/	A _____ works at a hotel check-in desk.	réceptionniste
shop assistant n	/'ʃɒp əsɪstənt/	A _____ serves customers in a shop.	vendeur/vendeuse
soldier n	/'səʊldʒə/	I'm a _____. I work for the army.	soldat
teacher n	/'tiːtʃə/	I'm a _____ I teach chemistry.	professeur, enseignant/enseignante
vet n	/vet/	I'm a ___. I look after animals.	vétérinaire
waiter n	/'weɪtə/	I am a _____ in a small café.	serveur
waitress n	/'weɪtrəs/	I work as a _____ in a restaurant.	serveuse

TIME

It's a quarter past six.	/ɪts ə 'kwɔːtə pɑːst sɪks/	_____Time to get up!	Il est six heures et quart.
It's a quarter to seven.	/ɪts ə 'kwɔːtə tə 'sevn/	What time is it? ~ _____	Il est sept heures moins le quart/moins quart. [Belgique]
It's five to seven.	/ɪts faɪv tə 'sevn/	_____ The bus will arrive soon.	Il est sept heures moins cinq.
It's half past six.	/ɪts hɑːf pɑːst sɪks/	What time is it? ~ _____	Il est six heures et demie.
It's six o'clock.	/ɪts sɪks əklɒk/	_____ I'm leaving the office now.	Il est six heures.
It's ten past six.	/ɪts ten pɑːst sɪks/	What time is it? ~ _____	Il est six heures dix.
It's three minutes past six.	/ɪts θriː 'mɪnɪts pɑːst sɪks/	What time is it? ~ _____	Il est six heures trois.
It's twenty past six.	/ɪts 'twenti pɑːst sɪks/	What time is it? ~ _____	Il est six heures vingt.
It's twenty-five to seven.	/ɪts 'twenti faɪv tə 'sevn/	What time is it? ~ _____	Il est sept heures moins vingt-cinq.

Useful words and phrases

call v	/kɔːl/	Are you Samantha? ~ Yes I am, but ___ me Sam.	appeler
Can I have a tea, please?	/kæn aɪ həv ə 'tiː pliːz/	_____ ~ To have here or take away?	Pouvez-vous me servir un thé, s'il vous plaît ?
Can I help you?	/kæn aɪ 'help ju/	_____ ~ A black coffee, please.	Que puis-je faire pour vous ?
change/changes v	/tʃeɪndʒ/tʃeɪndʒɪz/	Be careful because the weather _____ quickly.	changer/change
earn v	/ɜːn/	Does she ____ a lot of money?	gagner
feel v	/fiːl/	I ___ stupid when the waiter calls my name.	se sentir
finish/finishes v	/'fɪnɪʃ/fɪnɪʃɪz/	Our lessons _____ at 5 o'clock.	se terminer, finir
How interesting.	/haʊ 'ɪntrəstɪŋ/	I'm a singer. ~ Really? _____	C'est intéressant.
How many? det	/haʊ 'meni/	_____ children do you have?	Combien ?
How much is that?	/haʊ 'mʌtʃ ɪz ðæt/	_____ ~ That's £12.45, please.	Combien ça coûte ?
love/loves v	/lʌv/lʌvz/	British people ____ animals!	adorer/adore
Me too.	/'mi tuː/	I like classical music. ~ _____	Moi aussi.
need v	/niːd/	In the US you _____ ID when you buy a drink.	avoir besoin de
pay v	/peɪ/	You don't ___ when you take money out of an ATM.	payer
prefer v	/prɪ'fɜː/	I _____ the Starbucks in Britain.	préférer
rain/rains v	/reɪn/reɪnz/	_____ a lot so you'll need an umbrella.	pleuvoir/pleut
Really? adv	/'riːəli/	I'm a singer. ~ _____ How interesting.	Vraiment ?
sell v	/sel/	I ___ clothes in a shop.	vendre
To take away.	/tə teɪk ə'weɪ/	To have here or take away? ~ _____	À emporter.
travel v	/'trævl/	I _____ to lots of countries for my job.	voyager
walk v	/wɔːk/	Do you _____ to school? ~ No, I go by bus.	aller à pied
What about you?	/wɒt əbaʊt 'ju/	I'm hungry. _____	Et toi/vous ?
What time is it?	/wɒt 'taɪm ɪz ɪt/	_____ ~ It's nine fifteen.	Quelle heure est-il ?
What would you like?	/wɒt wəd ju 'laɪk/	_____ ~ A black coffee, please.	Que puis-je vous servir ?
What? det	/wɒt/	_____ do you do?	Que ?
What's the time?	/wɒts ðə 'taɪm/	_____ ~ It's six o'clock.	Quelle heure est-il ?
When? adv	/wen/	_____ do you go to the gym?	Quand ?
Where? adv	/weə/	_____ does he live?	Où ?
Which? det	/wɪtʃ/	In _____ picture can you see a cash machine?	Quel(e) ?
Why? adv	/waɪ/	_____ are you so tired?	Pourquoi ?

More words in File 3

barista n	/bə'rɪstə/	A _____ is a person who works in a coffee shop.	barman/barmaid
bird n	/bɜːd/	Look at that beautiful ____.	oiseau
brownie n	/'braʊni/	I'll have a coffee and a _____, please.	brownie
cakes pl n	/keɪks/	Can I have two chocolate _____ please?	gâteaux
cash machine (ATM) n	/kæʃ mə'ʃiːn/	Is there a _____ near here?	distributeur automatique de billets
coffee cup n	/'kɒfi kʌp/	Could you pass me a _____?	tasse à café

English File Elementary Third Edition English–French Wordlist © Oxford University Press 2012

comfortable adj	/ˈkʌmfətəbl/	I like it, it's nice and _____.	confortable
cyclist n	/ˈsaɪklɪst/	Chris Hoy is a British _____.	cycliste
driver n	/ˈdraɪvə/	Don't worry, I'm a good _____.	conducteur/conductrice
here adv	/hɪə/	Can we park ___?	ici
jacket n	/ˈdʒækɪt/	I wear a blue _____ and trousers and a white shirt and tie.	veste
nylon top n	/ˈnaɪlɒn tɒp/	My uniform is dark trousers and a white _____.	top en nylon, haut en nylon
pedestrian n	/pəˈdestriən/	Stop the car – there is a _____ on the zebra crossing.	piéton/piétonne
service n	/ˈsɜːvɪs/	The _____ is quick here.	service
shirt and tie n	/ʃɜːt ən ˈtaɪ/	I wear a blue jacket and trousers and a white _____.	chemise et cravate
skirt n	/skɜːt/	I sometimes wear a ____, but I prefer trousers.	jupe
sure adj	/ʃɔː/	I think we can park here, but I'm not ____.	sûr(e)
tie n	/taɪ/	I have to wear a shirt and __ at work.	cravate
trousers pl n	/ˈtraʊzəz/	I sometimes wear a skirt, but I prefer _____.	pantalon
turn n	/tɜːn/	It's your ____.	tour
word n	/wɜːd/	Complete the questions with a _____ or phrase from the list.	mot
work n	/wɜːk/	I drink coffee when I'm at _____.	travail
worker n	/ˈwɜːkə/	He is an office _____.	employé(e)
world n	/wɜːld/	Journalists work all over the _____.	monde
worry v	/ˈwʌri/	Don't _____. We have lots of time.	s'inquiéter
zebra crossing n	/ˌzebrə ˈkrɒsɪŋ/	When you walk on a _____ all the drivers stop.	passage pour piétons

File 4

Vocabulary Banks

THE FAMILY

aunt n	/ɑːnt/	My mum's sister, my _____ is two years older than she is.	tante
brother n	/ˈbrʌðə/	That's my _____ and his son.	frère
brother-in-law n	/ˈbrʌðər ɪn lɔː/	My _____ still lives with his parents.	beau-frère
children n	/ˈtʃɪldrən/	He has three _____, two boys and a girl.	enfants
cousin n	/ˈkʌzn/	My _____ goes to the same school as me.	cousin(e)
daughter n	/ˈdɔːtə/	My _____ is four years old.	fille
father n	/ˈfɑːðə/	My _____ is a doctor.	père
grandfather n	/ˈɡrænfɑːðə/	My _____ is 78 years old.	grand-père
grandmother n	/ˈɡrænmʌðə/	My _____ doesn't work.	grand-mère
mother-in-law n	/ˈmʌðər ɪn lɔː/	I don't like my _____.	belle-mère
nephew n	/ˈnefjuː/	My _____ is five years old.	neveu
niece n	/niːs/	I have got a nephew but not a ____.	nièce
parents pl n	/ˈpeərənts/	My _____ don't often listen to the radio.	parents
sister n	/ˈsɪstə/	My _____ has three children.	sœur
son n	/sʌn/	I have two daughters and a ___.	fils

stepfather n	/ˈstepfɑːðə/	Is he your father? ~ No, he's my _____	beau-père
stepsister n	/ˈstepsɪstə/	My _____ doesn't live with us.	demi-sœur
uncle n	/ˈʌŋkl/	I don't see my _____ very often.	oncle
wife n	/waɪf/	He lives in Chile with his ____.	femme

EVERYDAY ACTIVITIES

do exercise	/duː ˈeksəsaɪz/	I hardly ever _____.	faire de l'exercice
do homework	/duː ˈhəʊmwɜːk/	How often do you _____?	faire les devoirs
do the housework	/duː ðə ˈhaʊswɜːk/	I _____ on Saturday morning.	faire le ménage
finish work at 6.30	/fɪnɪʃ wɜːk ət sɪks ˈθɜːti/	I _____ p.m.	terminer le travail à 18 h 30
get dressed v	/get ˈdrest/	I have a shower, then I _____.	s'habiller
get home late	/get həʊm ˈleɪt/	They often _____.	rentrer tard à la maison
get up at 8.00	/get ʌp ət ˈeɪt/	I _____ a.m.	se lever à 8 h
go home early	/gəʊ həʊm ˈɜːli/	Sometimes I _____ from work.	rentrer tôt à la maison
go shopping	/gəʊ ˈʃɒpɪŋ/	I usually _____ at the weekend.	faire les courses
go to bed late	/gəʊ tə bed ˈleɪt/	I usually _____ on Friday.	se coucher tard
go to Italian classes	/gəʊ tə ɪˈtæliən klɑːsɪz/	I _____ twice a week.	prendre des cours d'italien
go to work by bus	/gəʊ tə wɜːk baɪ ˈbʌs/	We _____.	aller au travail en bus
have a bath	/hæv ə bɑːθ/	I don't like showers so I _____.	prendre un bain
have a coffee	/həv ə ˈkɒfi/	I _____ for breakfast.	prendre un café
have a shower v	/həv ə ˈʃaʊə/	I _____ every morning before breakfast.	prendre une douche
have breakfast	/həv ˈbrekfəst/	I like to _____ in bed at the weekends.	prendre le petit déjeuner
have lunch at work	/hæv lʌntʃ ət ˈwɜːk/	We _____, in the cafeteria.	déjeuner/dîner [Belgique, Suisse] au travail
have pizza for dinner	/hæv ˈpiːtsə fə dɪnə/	They often _____.	manger une pizza au dîner/au souper [Belgique, Suisse]
make the dinner	/meɪk ðə ˈdɪnə/	The children do their homework and I _____.	préparer le dîner/préparer le souper [Belgique, Suisse]
relax v	/rɪˈlæks/	I like to _____ at the weekend.	se détendre
sleep for eight hours	/sliːp fər eɪt ˈaʊəz/	They don't usually _____.	dormir huit heures
start work at 8.30	/stɑːt wɜːk ət eɪt ˈθɜːti/	I _____ a.m.	commencer le travail à 8 h 30
take the dog for a walk	/teɪk ðə dɒg fər ə ˈwɔːk/	I _____ every morning.	sortir le chien
wake up at 7.00	/weɪk ʌp ət ˈsevn/	I _____ a.m.	se réveiller à 7 h

ADVERBS AND EXPRESSIONS OF FREQUENCY

always adv	/ˈɔːlweɪz/	Why are you _____ late?	toujours
every (day/week/month/year) adv	/ˈevri/	They spend about 31 hours online _____.	chaque (jour/semaine/mois/année)
hardly ever adv	/ˈhɑːdli evə/	He _____ has breakfast.	presque jamais
never adv	/ˈnevə/	I _____ have time for breakfast.	jamais
normally adv	/ˈnɔːməli/	I _____ leave work at five.	d'habitude/normalement
often adv	/ˈɒfn/	He _____ has a hamburger for dinner.	souvent

once (a day/week/month/year) adv	/wʌns/	We go to the cinema _____.	une fois par (jour/semaine/mois/an)
only adv	/ˈəʊnli/	We ____ have half an hour for lunch.	seulement
sometimes adv	/ˈsʌmtaɪmz/	They're _____ late.	parfois
three times (a day/week/month/year) adv	/θriː taɪmz/	I play tennis _____.	trois fois par (jour/semaine/mois/an)
twice (a day/week/month/year) adv	/twaɪs/	I have English classes _____.	deux fois par (jour/semaine/mois/an)
usually adv	/ˈjuːʒuəli/	In the morning we _____ have five lessons.	habituellement

Useful words and phrases

after prep	/ˈɑːftə/	What do you do _____ work?	après
also adv	/ˈɔːlsəʊ/	They ____ have a good social life.	aussi
at prep	/æt/	I get up __ 7.30 a.m.	à
busy adj	/ˈbɪzi/	I work in a _____ restaurant.	animé(e)
everyone pron	/ˈevriwʌn/	Suddenly _____ arrives at the same time.	tout le monde
everything pron	/ˈevriθɪŋ/	I go back to the restaurant and check _____ is OK.	tout
for (a couple of hours) prep	/fə/	I go home to be with the family _____.	pendant (quelques heures)
have v	/hæv/	I always ____ toast for breakfast.	avoir, prendre
home n	/həʊm/	I go _____ to be with the family for a couple of hours.	maison
I don't enjoy it.	/aɪ dəʊnt ɪnˈdʒɔɪ ɪt/	I don't want to play golf because _____.	Ça ne me plaît pas.
job n	/dʒɒb/	I love my ___. I'm a teacher.	travail
own adj	/əʊn/	Nico is a chef and has his ____ restaurant.	propre
ready adj	/ˈredi/	I go to bed, _____ to start again the next day.	prêt(e)
relaxed adj	/rɪˈlækst/	He's a very _____ person.	détendu(e)
spend v	/spend/	How long does he _____ with the children?	passer
to prep	/tu/	I cycle __ work every day.	au, à, jusqu'à
up adv	/ʌp/	I live __ in the mountains.	en haut, en altitude
who pron	/huː/	Do you know ____ our teacher is?	qui

More words in File 4

approximately adv	/əˈprɒksɪmətli/	During his life he'll eat _____ 35,000 biscuits.	environ, approximativement
at least det	/ət ˈliːst/	All of my friends have _____ one TV in their house.	au moins
because conj	/bɪˈkɒz/	I never read the newspaper _____ I can't read very well.	parce que
contacts pl n	/ˈkɒntækts/	I have 100 _____ on my mobile phone.	contacts
factory n	/ˈfæktəri/	I work in a _____ that makes cars.	usine
four weeks pl n	/fɔː ˈwiːks/	_____ is equal to a month.	quatre semaines
healthy adj	/ˈhelθi/	I try to eat _____ food like fruit and vegetables.	sain(e)
house n	/haʊs/	I live in a _____ with my parents and sister.	maison
including prep	/ɪnˈkluːdɪŋ/	He can cook four dishes, _____ Spaghetti Bolognese.	y compris
less than det	/ˈles ðən/	It takes _____ ten minutes to walk to school from my house.	moins de

more than det	/ˈmɔː ðən/	He works _____ 40 hours a week.	plus de
royalty n	/ˈrɔɪəlti/	Our country doesn't have any _____. There is no king or queen.	royauté
seven days pl n	/ˈsevn deɪz/	_____ is equal to a week.	sept jours
sixty minutes pl n	/sɪksti ˈmɪnɪts/	_____ is equal to an hour.	soixante minutes
sixty seconds pl n	/sɪksti ˈsekəndz/	_____ is equal to a minute.	soixante secondes
sports player n	/spɔːts ˈpleɪə/	Messi is a very popular _____.	sportif/sportive
thirty minutes pl n	/θɜːti ˈmɪnɪts/	_____ is equal to half an hour.	trente minutes
twelve months pl n	/twelv ˈmʌnθs/	_____ is equal to a year.	douze mois
twenty-four hours pl n	/twenti fɔː ˈaʊəz/	_____ is equal to a day.	vingt-quatre heures
unemployed adj	/ˌʌnɪmˈplɔɪd/	I am _____ and haven't got a job.	sans emploi, au chômage

File 5

Vocabulary Banks

MORE VERB PHRASES

buy v	/baɪ/	You need to _____ a ticket before you get on the bus.	acheter
call/phone v	/kɔːl/fəʊn/	I want to _____ my mum.	appeler/téléphoner
dance v	/dɑːns/	I want to learn how to _____ the tango.	danser
draw v	/drɔː/	Can you _____ a picture of your house?	dessiner
drive v	/draɪv/	I _____ a Ferrari.	conduire
find v	/faɪnd/	It's hard to _____ a parking space on my street.	trouver
forget v	/fəˈget/	I always _____ my teacher's name!	oublier
give v	/gɪv/	The shop assistants _____ you good advice.	donner
hear v	/hɪə/	I can _____ a noise upstairs – is someone there?	entendre
help v	/help/	I _____ my children with their homework.	aider
look for phr v	/ˈlʊk fɔː/	I'll help you _____ your keys.	chercher
meet v	/miːt/	Nice to _____ you.	rencontrer
paint v	/peɪnt/	I want to _____ a picture of my father.	peindre
play v	/pleɪ/	You _____ tennis really well.	jouer
remember v	/rɪˈmembə/	There's our neighbour – can you _____ her name?	se rappeler
run v	/rʌn/	All the children _____ a race on Sports Day.	courir
see v	/siː/	I want to _____ a film this weekend.	voir
sing v	/sɪŋ/	Let's all _____ a song together!	chanter
swim v	/swɪm/	I like to _____ in the sea when I'm at the beach.	nager
take v	/teɪk/	I always _____ photos when I'm on holiday.	prendre
talk v	/tɔːk/	_____ to your teacher about your homework, please.	parler
tell v	/tel/	The waiters _____ jokes to make you laugh.	raconter
use v	/juːz/	I always _____ a computer at work.	utiliser
wait for phr v	/ˈweɪt fɔː/	I _____ a bus at the bus stop every morning.	attendre

THE WEATHER AND SEASONS

autumn n	/ˈɔːtəm/	In _____ the weather changes a lot.	automne
cloudy adj	/ˈklaʊdi/	In the summer it's sometimes sunny and sometimes _____.	nuageux/nuageuse
cold adj	/kəʊld/	Are you hot, Suzy? – No, I'm ____.	froid(e)
cool adj	/kuːl/	It's a bit ____ today – you should wear a jacket.	frais/fraîche
foggy adj	/ˈfɒgi/	London is a very ____ city because the air is really dirty.	il y a du brouillard
hot adj	/hɒt/	It's always very ___ in the summer in my country.	chaud/chaude
raining v	/ˈreɪnɪŋ/	Is it _____ outside?	pleuvoir
snowing v	/ˈsnəʊɪŋ/	It's _____ outside – let's go and make a snowman.	neiger
spring n	/sprɪŋ/	I love _____ here because all the flowers come out.	printemps
summer n	/ˈsʌmə/	The normal temperature in the _____ is 32°C.	été
sunny adj	/ˈsʌni/	Even in winter it can be _____ in the mornings here.	ensoleillé(e), il fait beau
warm adj	/wɔːm/	I love _____ weather so I always go to Egypt on holiday.	chaud(e)
windy adj	/ˈwɪndi/	It's really _____ today.	il y a du vent
winter n	/ˈwɪntə/	It often snows in the _____.	hiver

USEFUL WORDS AND PHRASES

argue v	/ˈɑːgjuː/	My parents _____ a lot.	se disputer
bank n	/bæŋk/	My sister works in a _____.	banque
bark v	/bɑːk/	Our dogs always _____ when they see a cat.	aboyer
cry v	/kraɪ/	The baby doesn't ___ very often.	pleurer
downstairs adv	/ˌdaʊnˈsteəz/	Two students live _____.	à l'étage du dessous
fly v	/flaɪ/	We ___ the flag when we go to an England football game.	arborer
happen v	/ˈhæpən/	What will _____ if you make a noise after 10.00 p.m.?	se passer
language n	/ˈlæŋgwɪdʒ/	What is this word in your _____?	langue
loud adj	/laʊd/	They play ____ music.	fort(e)
next door adv	/ˌnekst ˈdɔː/	My best friend lives _____ to me.	à côté
noisy adj	/ˈnɔɪzi/	They have _____ parties.	bruyant(e)
party n	/ˈpɑːti/	Do you want to come to my _____?	fête
shoes pl n	/ʃuːz/	I want to buy some new _____.	chaussures
shout v	/ʃaʊt/	Their children _____ all the time.	crier
start v	/stɑːt/	You can _____ when you're ready.	commencer
sweater n	/ˈswetə/	I'm cold – I think I'll put on a _____.	pull
think v	/θɪŋk/	What do you _____ they are doing now?	penser
T-shirt n	/ˈtiːʃɜːt/	I wear a _____ every day.	tee-shirt
upstairs adv	/ˌʌpˈsteəz/	I live in this flat, and an old woman lives _____.	à l'étage du dessus
young adj	/jʌŋ/	Your dad looks really _____.	jeune

More words in File 5

album n	/ˈælbəm/	She has a new _____ coming soon.	album
audience n	/ˈɔːdiəns/	He will only play for a small _____.	public
concert n	/ˈkɒnsət/	I'm watching a _____ in a theatre in London.	concert
copy n	/ˈkɒpi/	Do you have a _____ of her new album?	exemplaire
Don't be silly!	/dəʊnt bi ˈsɪli/	_____ – I'm not angry with you.	Ne sois/Ne soyez pas stupide !
Have fun!	/hæv ˈfʌn/	_____ Don't be home too late.	Amuse-toi/Amusez-vous bien !
hit n	/hɪt/	I love her latest ____ It always plays on the radio.	hit
I have to go.	/aɪ həv tə ˈgəʊ/	_____ See you tomorrow.	Je dois y aller.
It's so cool!	/ɪts səʊ ˈkuːl/	I love your new bag! _____	Il est cool !
No problem.	/nəʊ ˈprɒbləm/	_____ I can help you any time.	Pas de problème.
No way!	/nəʊ ˈweɪ/	_____ You can't have my jacket!	Pas question !
number 1 n	/nʌmbə ˈwʌn/	Her song is now _____.	numéro 1
recording contract n	/rɪˈkɔːdɪŋ ˈkɒntrækt/	She has a _____ with Epic Records.	contrat avec une maison de disque
Right now?	/raɪt ˈnaʊ/	Can you help me? ~ _____	Maintenant ?
single n	/ˈsɪŋgl/	You can buy her new _____ tomorrow.	single
That's OK.	/ðæts əʊˈkeɪ/	_____ I can ask Jason for help.	Ce n'est pas grave.
top ten n	/ˌtɒp ˈten/	He wants a _____ record in the USA next year.	parmi les dix meilleurs
version n	/ˈvɜːʒn/	She sings a new _____ of a Leonard Cohen song.	version
Wait a minute.	/weɪt ə ˈmɪnɪt/	_____ I can't find my keys.	Attends/Attendez une minute.
What can you play?	/wɒt kən ju ˈpleɪ/	_____ ~ I can play the guitar.	Quel instrument joues-tu/jouez-vous ?
What's wrong?	/wɒts ˈrɒŋ/	_____ You look sad.	Qu'est-ce qui ne va pas ?

File 6

Vocabulary Banks

THE DATE

January n	/ˈdʒænjuəri/	In the UK _____ is a cold and dark month.	janvier
February n	/ˈfebruəri/	Valentine's Day is in _____.	février
March n	/mɑːtʃ/	Easter Sunday is a Christian holiday in _____ or April.	mars
April n	/ˈeɪprəl/	Easter Sunday is a Christian holiday in March or _____.	avril
May n	/meɪ/	Paul's favourite month is _____ because the weather is warm.	mai
June n	/dʒuːn/	My sister's birthday's in _____.	juin
July n	/dʒuˈlaɪ/	My birthday's in _____	juillet
August n	/ˈɔːgəst/	My favourite month is _____ because it's usually hot.	août
September n	/sepˈtembə/	I usually take holidays in _____.	septembre
October n	/ɒkˈtəʊbə/	_____ is a cold month.	octobre
November n	/nəʊˈvembə/	Halloween is in _____.	novembre
December n	/dɪˈsembə/	Christmas Day is in _____.	décembre

1st (first) det	/fɜːst/	Saturday is the ____ day when I can stay in bed until noon!	1er (premier)
2nd (second) det	/ˈsekənd/	This is my ____ English lesson.	2e (deuxième)
3rd (third) det	/θɜːd/	The ____ Monday in January is the most depressing day of the year.	3e (troisième)
4th (fourth) det	/fɔːθ/	My birthday is the ____ of December.	4e (quatrième)
5th (fifth) det	/fɪfθ/	This is the ____ time I have seen this movie.	5e (cinquième)
6th (sixth) det	/sɪksθ/	That is the ____ goal in the game.	6e (sixième)
7th (seventh) det	/ˈsevnθ/	My sister's birthday is the ____ of January.	7e (septième)
8th (eighth) det	/eɪtθ/	My mum's birthday is the ____ of March.	8e (huitième)
9th (ninth) det	/naɪnθ/	It's the ____ of June today.	9e (neuvième)
10th (tenth) det	/tenθ/	This is my ____ birthday.	10e (dixième)
11th (eleventh) det	/ɪˈlevnθ/	My birthday is the ____ of August.	11e (onzième)
12th (twelfth) det	/twelfθ/	It's the ____ of April.	12e (douzième)
13th (thirteenth) det	/θɜːˈtiːnθ/	Friday the ____ is an unlucky day for some people.	13e (treizième)
14th (fourteenth) det	/fɔːˈtiːnθ/	My birthday is the ____ of October.	14e (quatorzième)
20th (twentieth) det	/ˈtwentiəθ/	Easter is the ____ of April this year.	20e (vingtième)
21st (twenty-first) det	/twenti ˈfɜːst/	It's my ____ birthday today.	21e (vingt et unième)
22nd (twenty-second) det	/twenti ˈsekənd/	It's her ____ birthday.	22e (vingt-deuxième)
23rd (twenty-third) det	/twenti ˈθɜːd/	My dad's birthday is the ____ of February.	23e (vingt-troisième)
24th (twenty-fourth) det	/twenti ˈfɔːθ/	Christmas Eve is the ____ of December.	24e (vingt-quatrième)
30th (thirtieth) det	/ˈθɜːtiəθ/	Happy ____ birthday!	25e (vingt-cinquième)
31st (thirty-first) det	/θɜːti ˈfɜːst/	New Year's Eve is the ____ of December.	31e (trente et unième)

Useful words and phrases

asleep adj	/əˈsliːp/	I like getting up early when other people are ____.	endormi(e)
blues n	/bluːz/	My dad likes ____.	blues
classical adj	/ˈklæsɪkl/	Ben doesn't like ____ music.	classique
concert hall n	/ˈkɒnsət ˈhɔːl/	An orchestra is playing in the ____.	salle de concert
conductor n	/kənˈdʌktə/	Dudamel is the ____ of the Los Angeles Philharmonic orchestra.	chef d'orchestre
fall v	/fɔːl/	Be careful – don't ____.	tomber
heavy metal n	/ˌhevi ˈmetl/	Colin likes ____.	heavy metal/hard rock
hip hop n	/ˈhɪp hɒp/	I don't like ____ music.	hip-hop
in a good mood	/ɪn ə gʊd ˈmuːd/	I love Christmas because everyone is ____.	de bonne humeur
Latin adj	/ˈlætɪn/	I like ____ music.	latino
leave v	/liːv/	I ____ for work at 9.00 a.m.	partir
orchestra n	/ˈɔːkɪstrə/	Inside the concert hall a top ____ is playing brilliantly.	orchestre
pick v	/pɪk/	Can you help me ____ some flowers for our teacher?	choisir
pick up phr v	/pɪk ˈʌp/	____ the phone, please.	décrocher
practise v	/ˈpræktɪs/	____ saying the words.	s'entraîner
put down phr v	/pʊt ˈdaʊn/	Stop writing and ____ your pens.	poser
R&B n	/ˌɑːr ən ˈbiː/	I like rock, but I don't like ____.	R&B
reggae n	/ˈregeɪ/	She loves ____.	reggae

ring n	/rɪŋ/	He is going to give her a ____ for her birthday.	bague
rock n	/rɒk/	I like ____, but I don't like R&B.	rock
smile v	/smaɪl/	You will feel better if you ____.	sourire
stay in bed	/steɪ ɪn 'bed/	On Saturday I _____ until noon.	rester au lit
tonight n	/tə'naɪt/	I want to wear it _____.	ce soir
vegetable n	/'vedʒtəbl/	What's your favourite _____	légume
What's your favourite...?	/wɒts jɔː 'feɪvərɪt.../	_____ time of day?	Quel est votre...préféré(e) ?

More words in File 6

biography n	/baɪ'ɒgrəfi/	I'm reading a _____ about my favourite actor.	biographie
amusing adj	/ə'mjuːzɪŋ/	The bus drivers tell interesting and _____ stories.	amusant(e)
awful adj	/'ɔːfl/	That song's _____ – can you turn it off?	affreux/affreuse
band n	/bænd/	Do you play in a ____?	groupe
blow v	/bləʊ/	My soup is too hot. ~ You should _____ on it.	souffler
don't like	/dəʊnt 'laɪk/	I like rock, but I _____ R&B.	n'aime pas
don't mind	/dəʊnt 'maɪnd/	I _____ getting up early.	ne me dérange pas
fantastic adj	/fæn'tæstɪk/	I think they're _____.	fantastique
film n	/fɪlm/	What is your favourite ___?	film
great adj	/greɪt/	I think they're _____.	super
greet v	/griːt/	Local people _____ you like an old friend.	accueillir
guide n	/gaɪd/	Our tourist _____ is really friendly.	guide
hate v	/heɪt/	I ____ getting up early.	détester
I think they're...	/aɪ 'θɪŋk ðeə.../	_____ great.	Je pense qu'ils/elles sont...
main adj	/meɪn/	They stop at all the _____ tourist attractions.	principal(e)
message n	/'mesɪdʒ/	Can you give a _____ to him?	message
neighbour n	/'neɪbə/	My _____ is very friendly.	voisin(e)
not bad adj	/nɒt 'bæd/	It's _____. I quite like it.	pas mauvais/pas mauvaise
now adv	/naʊ/	In Venezuela ____ it's cooler to like Strauss than salsa.	maintenant
romantic novel n	/rəʊ'mæntɪk nɒvl/	At the moment Anya is reading a _____.	roman romantique
shine v	/ʃaɪn/	The sun doesn't often _____ in January.	briller
snowy adj	/'snəʊi/	It's cold and _____ outside.	neigeux/neigeuse
student n	/'stjuːdnt/	She's a _____ at university.	étudiant(e)
terrible adj	/'terəbl/	This food is _____.	horrible
trilogy n	/'trɪlədʒi/	There are three books in a _____.	trilogie
viola n	/vi'əʊlə/	I can play the _____ and the piano.	alto
wet adj	/wet/	It's really ___ in England.	humide
yacht n	/jɒt/	He sails his _____ on the sea.	yacht
yoga n	/'jəʊgə/	I like doing _____	yoga

File 7

Vocabulary Banks

GO, HAVE, GET

get a newspaper	/ˈnjuːzpeɪpə/	Can you _____ while you're out?	acheter un journal
get a taxi/a bus/a train	/ˈtæksi/bʌs/treɪn/	Don't walk home – you should _____.	prendre un taxi/un bus/un train
get an email/letter	/ˈiːmeɪl/ˈletə/	Did you _____ from Mike yesterday?	recevoir un e-mail/une lettre
get dressed v	/drest/	I have a shower, then I _____.	s'habiller
get home	/həʊm/	I usually _____ at about 6.30 p.m.	rentrer à la maison
get to the airport	/ˈeəpɔːt/	It's best to _____ two hours before your flight.	arriver à l'aéroport
get up (early) phr v	/ʌp/	I have to _____ early most days.	se lever (tôt)
go back (to work) phr v	/bæk/	It's difficult to _____ to work after a holiday.	retourner (au travail)
go by bus/by car/by plane	/bʌs/kɑː/pleɪn/	I sometimes walk to work, but I prefer to _____.	aller en bus/en voiture/en avion
go for a walk	/wɔːk/	Let's _____ in the park.	aller se promener
go home (from school)	/həʊm/	I _____ by bike.	rentrer à la maison (après l'école)
go on holiday	/ˈhɒlədeɪ/	I want to _____ to Mexico.	partir en vacances
go out phr v	/aʊt/	I always _____ with my best friends on Friday night.	sortir
go shopping	/ˈʃɒpɪŋ/	I usually _____ at the weekend.	faire les courses
go to a restaurant	/ˈrestrɒnt/	Shall we _____ tonight?	aller au restaurant
go to bed	/bed/	I'm always tired because _____ late.	se coucher
go to church/to mosque	/tʃɜːtʃ/mɒsk/	I _____ on Sundays with my grandparents.	aller à l'église/à la mosquée
go to the beach	/biːtʃ/	It's a beautiful, sunny day – let's _____.	aller à la plage
have a car/a bike	/kɑː/baɪk/	I _____. It's dark blue.	avoir une voiture/un vélo
have a drink	/drɪŋk/	Shall we _____ in the bar before we go home?	boire un verre
have a good time	/ɡʊd ˈtaɪm/	I always _____ when I go out with Chris.	passer un bon moment
have a sandwich	/ˈsænwɪdʒ/	I usually _____ for lunch.	manger un sandwich
have a shower/a bath/a swim	/ˈʃaʊə/bɑːθ/swɪm/	I _____ every morning before breakfast.	prendre une douche/prendre un bain/se baigner
have long hair	/lɒŋ ˈheə/	You ____ really _____.	avoir les cheveux longs

Useful words and phrases

artist n	/ˈɑːtɪst/	Van Gogh was a brilliant _____.	artiste
a year ago	/ə ˈjɜːr əɡəʊ/	I finished university _____.	il y a un an
businessman/businesswoman n	/ˈbɪznəsmæn/ˈbɪznəswʊmən/	My uncle is a rich _____.	homme/femme d'affaires
composer n	/kəmˈpəʊzə/	Mozart was an excellent _____.	compositeur/compositrice
film director n	/fɪlm dəˈrektə/	She has two children with her partner Tim Burton, a _____.	réalisateur/réalisatrice
five minutes ago	/faɪv ˈmɪnɪts əɡəʊ/	The train left _____.	il y a cinq minutes
in 2009	/ɪn tuː θaʊznd ən ˈnaɪn/	They got married _____.	en 2009
inventor n	/ɪnˈventə/	My brother wants to be an _____ when he leaves school.	inventeur/inventrice

last month	/lɑːst ˈmʌnθ/	I went to Germany _____.	le mois dernier
last night	/lɑːst ˈnaɪt/	We watched a good film on TV _____.	hier soir
last summer	/lɑːst ˈsʌmə/	We went to Italy _____.	l'été dernier
last week	/lɑːst ˈwiːk/	I watched a really good film _____.	la semaine dernière, passée [Suisse]
novelist n	/ˈnɒvəlɪst/	Emily Brontë is a famous English _____.	romancier/romancière
painter n	/ˈpeɪntə/	My father's a _____.	peintre
poet n	/ˈpəʊɪt/	He was an excellent sportsman, and was also a ____.	poète/poétesse
sailor n	/ˈseɪlə/	My grandfather was a _____.	marin
scientist n	/ˈsaɪəntɪst/	Charles Darwin was a _____.	scientifique
singer n	/ˈsɪŋə/	Shakira's a _____.	chanteur/chanteuse
the day before yesterday	/ðə deɪ bɪfɔː ˈjestədeɪ/	I went shopping in town _____.	avant-hier
three days ago	/θriː ˈdeɪz əgəʊ/	I last saw Rebecca _____.	il y a trois jours
writer n	/ˈraɪtə/	He was an English _____.	écrivain
yesterday morning	/jestədeɪ ˈmɔːnɪŋ/	Where were you at 8 o'clock _____?	hier matin

More words in File 7

at the traffic lights prep	/ət ðə ˈtræfɪk laɪts/	Turn right _____.	au feu de signalisation
bridge n	/brɪdʒ/	There's a _____ near my house.	pont
Can you...?	/ˈkæn ju.../	_____ tell me the way to Tate Modern?	Peux-tu/Pouvez-vous... ?
Could you...?	/ˈkəd ju.../	_____ say that again please?	Pourrais-tu/Pourriez-vous... ?
Excuse me, please. Where's the...?	/ɪkˈskjuːs miː pliːz weəz ðə.../	_____ nearest supermarket?	Excuse/Excusez-moi, où est le/la... ?
go past	/gəʊ pɑːst/	_____ the library.	passer devant
go straight on	/gəʊ streɪt ɒn/	_____ down this road.	continuer tout droit
Maybe another time?	/ˈmeɪbi əˈnʌðər taɪm/	_____ I'm a bit too tired today.	Peut-être une autre fois ?
on the corner	/ɒn ðə ˈkɔːnə/	There's a shop _____ of this road.	à l'angle
roundabout n	/ˈraʊndəbaʊt/	There's a _____ on this road.	rond-point
turn left	/tɜːn ˈleft/	_____ at the end of this street.	tourner à gauche
turn right	/tɜːn ˈraɪt/	_____ at the traffic lights.	tourner à droite
What is there to see?	/wɒt ɪz ðeər tə ˈsiː/	_____ in your hometown?	Qu'y a-t-il à voir ?
What would you like to visit?	/wɒt wəd ju laɪk tə ˈvɪzɪt/	_____ when you come to stay with me?	Que souhaiterais-tu visiter ?
When was the last time you...?	/ˈwen wɒz ðə lɑːst taɪm ju.../	_____ went on holiday?	À quand remontent tes/vos derniers/dernières... ?
Wow. What a [view]!	/ˈwaʊ wɒt ə ˈvjuː/	_____ Your house is amazing!	Ouah. Quelle [vue] !

File 8

Vocabulary Banks

THE HOUSE

air conditioning n	/ˈeə kəndɪʃnɪŋ/	Is there central heating or _____?	climatisation
armchair n	/ˈɑːmtʃeə/	There are two sofas and an _____.	fauteuil
balcony n	/ˈbælkəni/	Is there a _____?	balcon
bath n	/bɑːθ/	I had a ____ and went to bed.	bain
bathroom n	/ˈbɑːθruːm/	Is there a shower in the _____?	salle de bain/salle de bains
bed n	/bed/	Each bedroom has a ___, a desk, and a wardrobe.	lit
bedroom n	/ˈbedruːm/	This is the biggest _____ in the house.	chambre
carpet n	/ˈkɑːpɪt/	Is there a _____ on the floor?	tapis
ceiling n	/ˈsiːlɪŋ/	Be careful. The _____ is very low here.	plafond
central heating n	/ˌsentrəl ˈhiːtɪŋ/	Is there _____ in the house?	chauffage central
cooker n	/ˈkʊkə/	There is a _____ in the kitchen.	cuisinière
cupboard n	/ˈkʌbəd/	Do you keep these glasses in a _____?	placard
dining room n	/ˈdaɪnɪŋ ruːm/	Where is the _____?	salle à manger
fireplace n	/ˈfaɪəpleɪs/	There is a _____ in the living room.	cheminée
floor n	/flɔː/	Is there a carpet on the ____?	sol
fridge n	/frɪdʒ/	There is a _____ in the kitchen.	réfrigérateur
garage n	/ˈɡærɪdʒ/	Oh yes, there's a big _____ over there.	garage
garden n	/ˈɡɑːdn/	I went for a walk in the _____.	jardin
hall n	/hɔːl/	Put your coats in the ___.	hall
kitchen n	/ˈkɪtʃɪn/	Alison likes her _____ because she can eat there.	cuisine
lamp n	/læmp/	There is a ____ on the table.	lampe
light n	/laɪt/	Is there a ____ in this room?	lumière
living room n	/ˈlɪvɪŋ ruːm/	This is the _____ It's quite big and it's very light.	salon
mirror n	/ˈmɪrə/	There is a _____ above the fireplace.	miroir, glace
plant n	/plɑːnt/	There is a ____ in the living room.	plante
shelf (shelves) n	/ʃelf/	I have a ____ for books and DVDs.	étagère
shower n	/ˈʃaʊə/	I have a _____ in the morning.	douche
sofa/couch n	/ˈsəʊfə/kaʊtʃ/	There is a ___ and an armchair.	canapé
stairs pl n	/steəz/	The ____ are over there – let's go upstairs.	escalier
study n	/ˈstʌdi/	Jane has a good view from her _____	bureau
toilet n	/ˈtɔɪlət/	Is there _____ downstairs?	toilettes, toilette [Belgique]
wall n	/wɔːl/	I sit next to the ___.	mur
washing machine n	/ˈwɒʃɪŋ məʃiːn/	I have four children so I need a _____.	machine à laver

PREPOSITIONS: PLACE AND MOVEMENT

behind prep	/bɪˈhaɪnd/	I couldn't sleep on the plane because of the children _____ me.	derrière
between prep	/bɪˈtwiːn/	The bank is _____ the cinema and the post office.	entre
down prep	/daʊn/	I saw a ghost coming _____ the stairs.	vers le bas
from...to prep	/frəm...tu/	There is a secret tunnel that goes _____ the fireplace _ Room 11.	depuis...jusqu'à
in prep	/ɪn/	Who are the ghosts _ the two hotels?	dans
in front of prep	/ɪn ˈfrʌnt əv/	There is a shop _____ the school.	en face de
into prep	/ˈɪntu/	Come _____ the library with me, please.	dans
next to prep	/ˈnekst tə/	Yes, there was. It was _____ the window.	à côté de
on prep	/ɒn/	They saw a young woman sitting _ the bed.	sur
opposite prep	/ˈɒpəzɪt/	I live _____ a bus stop.	en face
out of prep	/ˈaʊt əv/	Get _____ bed – it's 11 o'clock!	hors du, sortir de
over prep	/ˈəʊvə/	Go _____ the hill to get to the garage.	là-bas
towards prep	/təˈwɔːdz/	Walk _____ the library and then turn right.	vers
under prep	/ˈʌndə/	I put my bag _____ my seat.	sous
up prep	/ʌp/	Your room is _ the stairs on the left.	vers le haut

Useful words and phrases

ago adv	/əˈgəʊ/	We went to Istanbul three years _____.	auparavant, il y a…
beer n	/bɪə/	My favourite drink is _____.	bière
building n	/ˈbɪldɪŋ/	Is there a _____ in your town that people think is haunted?	bâtiment
careful adj	/ˈkeəfl/	Be _____. The ceiling is very low here.	prudent(e)
crime n	/kraɪm/	There isn't much _____ in my city. It's very safe.	criminalité
dear n	/dɪə/	Call me Barbara, _____.	mon cher/ma chère
detective n	/dɪˈtektɪv/	He wrote stories about a brilliant _____ Sherlock Holmes.	détective
ear n	/ɪə/	My _____ hurts.	oreille
enemy n	/ˈenəmi/	She was not my friend, she was my _____.	ennemi(e)
ghost n	/gəʊst/	When I saw the man standing there, I thought he was a _____.	fantôme
guest n	/gest/	There was only one other _____ in the hotel.	client
heating n	/ˈhiːtɪŋ/	Is there central _____ in the house?	chauffage
kill v	/kɪl/	Listen, inspector, I did not _____ Jeremy.	tuer
lounge n	/laʊndʒ/	One night a lot of books fell off a shelf in the _____.	salon
owner n	/ˈəʊnə/	Rod Davies is the _____ of the hotel.	propriétaire
patient n	/ˈpeɪʃnt/	The doctor told his _____ to do more exercise.	patient(e)
short story n	/ˌʃɔːt ˈstɔːri/	He wrote his first _____ when he was a student.	nouvelle
suite n	/swiːt/	The hotel has 50 rooms and one _____.	suite

File 9

Vocabulary Banks

FOOD

apples *pl n*	/ˈæplz/	Can I have some _____ please?	pommes
bananas *pl n*	/bəˈnɑːnəz/	_____ are my favourite fruit.	bananes
biscuits *pl n*	/ˈbɪskɪts/	How many _____ did you eat?	biscuits
bread *n*	/bred/	How much _____ do you eat a day?	pain
breakfast *n*	/ˈbrekfəst/	For _____ I had an enormous cup of espresso.	petit-déjeuner
butter *n*	/ˈbʌtə/	How much _____ do you use?	beurre
carrots *pl n*	/ˈkærəts/	_____ are about five per cent sugar.	carottes
cereal *n*	/ˈsɪəriəl/	I have a cup of tea and _____ for breakfast.	céréales
cheese *n*	/tʃiːz/	We had a snack – _____ and biscuits.	fromage
chips (French fries) *pl n*	/tʃɪps (ˌfrentʃ ˈfraɪz)/	We're having fish and _____ for dinner.	frites
chocolate *n*	/ˈtʃɒklət/	How much _____ do you eat?	chocolat
coffee *n*	/ˈkɒfi/	For breakfast I had an enormous cup of _____.	café
crisps *pl n*	/krɪsps/	A packet of _____ has approximately 0.3 grammes of salt.	chips
desserts *pl n*	/dɪˈzɜːts/	I prefer _____ to starters.	desserts
fish *n*	/fɪʃ/	_____ is my favourite food.	poisson
fruit *n*	/fruːt/	Bananas are my favourite _____.	fruit
fruit salad *n*	/fruːt ˈsæləd/	You can make some _____ for dessert.	salade de fruits
ice cream *n*	/aɪs ˈkriːm/	I'd like some vanilla _____ for dessert.	crème glacée, glace
jam *n*	/dʒæm/	I like _____ on my toast.	confiture
lettuce *n*	/ˈletɪs/	I need to buy a _____, some tomatoes, and a cucumber.	laitue
lunch/dinner *n*	/lʌntʃ/ˈdɪnə/	We're having pizza for _____ tonight.	déjeuner/dîner dîner/souper [Belgique]
meat (steak, chicken, sausages, ham) *n*	/miːt (steɪk, ˈtʃɪkɪn, ˈsɒsɪdʒɪz, hæm)/	I'm a vegetarian, so I don't eat any _____.	viande (steak, poulet, saucisses, jambon)
milk *n*	/mɪlk/	Do your children drink any _____?	lait
mushrooms *pl n*	/ˈmʌʃrʊmz/	I had fish and vegetables – _____ and tomatoes.	champignons
(olive) oil *n*	/(ˈɒlɪv) ɔɪl/	A bottle of olive _____ doesn't have any salt.	huile (d'olive)
onions *pl n*	/ˈʌnjənz/	I had grilled fish with vegetables – peppers and _____	oignons
(orange) juice *n*	/(ˈɒrɪndʒ) dʒuːs/	How much orange _____ is there in that carton?	jus (d'orange)
oranges *pl n*	/ˈɒrɪndʒɪz/	_____ are very good for you.	oranges
pasta *n*	/ˈpæstə/	_____ is from Italy.	pâtes
peas *pl n*	/piːz/	My daughter loves _____.	petits pois
pineapple *n*	/ˈpaɪnæpl/	Can you please get a _____ at the supermarket?	ananas
potatoes *pl n*	/pəˈteɪtəʊz/	Are there any _____?	pommes de terre
rice *n*	/raɪs/	I had grilled fish with some brown _____ and vegetables.	riz

salad n	/ˈsæləd/	I'd like the mozzarella ____ and then the chicken, please.	salade
sandwich n	/ˈsænwɪdʒ/	A cheese and tomato _____, please.	sandwich
snacks pl n	/snæks/	I eat three meals a day, and no _____.	en-cas
strawberries pl n	/ˈstrɔːbəriz/	Oranges are healthier than _____	fraises
sugar n	/ˈʃʊgə/	Are you sure this is salt? I think it's _____.	sucre
sweets pl n	/swiːts/	I eat quite a lot of _____.	bonbons
tea n	/tiː/	British people drink a lot of ___.	thé
toast n	/təʊst/	I had some cereal and fruit, and a piece of ____.	toast, pain grillé
tomatoes pl n	/təˈmɑːtəʊz/	I had fish and vegetables – mushrooms and _____	tomates

HIGH NUMBERS

105 a/one hundred and five	/əˌwʌn ˈhʌndrəd ən faɪv/	I live at number ____.	105 cent cinq
200 two hundred	/tuː ˈhʌndrəd/	You need ____ grammes of sugar for this cake.	200 deux cents
350 three hundred and fifty	/θriː ˈhʌndrəd ən ˈfɪfti/	You need ____ grammes of flour.	350 trois cent cinquante
875 eight hundred and seventy-five	/eɪt ˈhʌndrəd ən sevnti ˈfaɪv/	There are ____ students in our school.	875 huit cent soixante-quinze, septante-cinq [Belgique, Suisse]
1,000 a/one thousand	/əˌwʌn ˈθaʊznd/	There are _____ people in my village.	1 000 mille
1,500 one thousand five hundred	/əˌwʌn ˈθaʊznd faɪv ˈhʌndrəd/	There are _____ people working for this company.	1 500 mille cinq cents
2,012 two thousand and twelve	/tuː ˈθaʊznd ən ˈtwelv/	There are _____ students at my university.	2 012 deux mille douze
5,420 five thousand four hundred and twenty	/faɪv ˈθaʊznd fɔː hʌndrəd ən ˈtwenti/	About _____ people live in my home town.	5 420 cinq mille quatre cent vingt
25,000 twenty-five thousand	/twenti faɪv ˈθaʊznd/	About _____ people live in my city.	25 000 vingt-cinq mille
100,000 a/one hundred thousand	/əˌwʌn hʌndrəd ˈθaʊznd/	The biggest football stadium in my country holds _____ people.	100 000 cent mille
1,000,000 a/one million	/əˌwʌn ˈmɪljən/	About _____ people live in my city.	1 000 000 un million
2,300,000 two million three hundred thousand	/tuː ˈmɪljən θriː hʌndrəd ˈθaʊznd/	My country is quite small – _____ people live there.	2 300 000 deux millions trois cent mille

USEFUL WORDS AND PHRASES

a little det	/ə ˈlɪtl/	I had an enormous cup of espresso with _____ cream.	un peu de
a lot det	/ə ˈlɒt/	I eat ____ of fish.	beaucoup
approximate adj	/əˈprɒksɪmət/	What is the _____ population of the UK?	approximatif/approximative
bacon n	/ˈbeɪkən/	I had a bowl of pasta with chorizo and _____.	bacon, lard [Suisse]
bottle n	/bɒtl/	A _____ of mineral water, please.	bouteille
bowl n	/bəʊl/	I had a ____ of pasta with chorizo and bacon.	bol
breast (chicken) n	/brest (ˈtʃɪkɪn)/	I had a grilled chicken _____ and vegetables.	blanc (de poulet)
can n	/kæn/	A ___ of cola has approximately 35g of sugar.	canette
carton n	/kɑːtn/	I drink a _____ of orange juice every week.	brique
centre n	/ˈsentə/	The information _____ is next to the reception.	centre
cinema n	/ˈsɪnəmə/	I go to the _____ once every week.	cinéma
delicious adj	/dɪˈlɪʃəs/	Let's try your soup. Mmm, that's _____.	délicieux/délicieuse

dish n	/dɪʃ/	In the evening I had a vegetarian pasta ____.	plat
fast food n	/ˌfɑːst 'fuːd/	_____ is not very healthy.	restauration rapide/fast-food
fresh adj	/freʃ/	If an egg floats in a cup of water, it isn't very ____.	frais/fraîche
grilled adj	/grɪld/	I had a _____ chicken breast and vegetables.	grillé(e)
information n	/ˌɪnfə'meɪʃn/	Read the _____ and answer the questions.	informations
jar n	/dʒɑː/	I bought a ___ of strawberry jam from the market.	pot
meal n	/miːl/	Breakfast is my favourite _____.	repas
none pron	/nʌn/	How many vegetables do you eat? ~ _____. I don't like them.	aucun(e)
packet n	/'pækɪt/	I bought a _____ of rice.	paquet
pepper n	/'pepə/	We need a red _____ for this recipe.	poivron
popcorn n	/'pɒpkɔːn/	First I had a glass of sherry and a bowl of _____.	pop-corn
population n	/ˌpɒpju'leɪʃn/	What is the approximate _____ of the UK?	population
quite a lot det	/kwaɪt ə 'lɒt/	There's _____ of salt in bread.	vraiment beaucoup, pas mal
salt n	/sɔːlt/	I don't put much ___ on my food.	sel
sauce n	/sɔːs/	I had a bowl of pasta in tomato _____.	sauce
science n	/'saɪəns/	I love _____. I find it more interesting than history.	science
special adj	/'speʃl/	I'm not doing anything _____ this weekend.	spécial
steak n	/steɪk/	I had _____ and chips for dinner.	steak
sweetcorn n	/'swiːtkɔːn/	I had fish and vegetables – _____ and tomatoes.	maïs doux
takeaway n	/'teɪkəweɪ/	I got _____ sushi from a restaurant called Itsu.	à emporter
tin n	/tɪn/	We need a ___ of tuna for this recipe.	boîte de conserve
tuna n	/'tjuːnə/	How many tins of ____ do we have?	thon

More words in File 9

Are you ready to order?	/ɑː ju redi tə 'ɔːdə/	_____ ~ Yes, we are.	Êtes-vous prêt/prête(s) à passer la commande ?
beat v	/biːt/	Do you think Pat will ____ the other contestants?	battre
calories pl n	/'kæləriz/	How many _____ are there in a hamburger?	calories
chorizo n	/tʃə'riːzəʊ/	_____ is a kind of Spanish sausage.	chorizo
Come this way, please.	/kʌm ðɪs weɪ 'pliːz/	_____ Your table's over here.	Suivez-moi, s'il vous plaît.
competition n	/ˌkɒmpə'tɪʃn/	During the _____ he answered several difficult questions.	compétition
Congratulations!	/kənˌgrætʃu'leɪʃnz/	_____ You passed your driving test!	Félicitations !
contestant n	/kən'testənt/	Would you like to be a _____ on a quiz show?	candidat(e)
Could we have the bill, please?	/kəd wi hæv ðə 'bɪl pliːz/	_____ ~ Certainly, one moment please.	Pourrions-nous avoir l'addition s'il vous plaît ?
course n	/kɔːs/	You have to cook three dishes, a starter, a main _____ and a dessert.	plat
final n	/'faɪnl/	Is that your ____ answer?	final(e), définitif/définitive
general knowledge n	/dʒenrəl 'nɒlɪdʒ/	The contestants answer _____ questions.	culture générale
Go ahead.	/gəʊ ə'hed/	Can I ask him? ~ Yes. _____	Vas-y/Allez-y.
Good evening. Do you have a...?	/gʊd 'iːvnɪŋ də ju həv ə.../	_____ table for two?	Bonsoir. Avez-vous un(e)... ?
Good luck!	/gʊd 'lʌk/	I have my driving test tomorrow. ~ _____	Bonne chance !
Good news?	/gʊd 'njuːz/	_____ ~ Yes, she said yes!	Bonne nouvelle ?

Happy birthday!	/ˈhæpi ˈbɜːθdeɪ/	_____ How old are you now?	Joyeux anniversaire !
home-made adj	/ˌhəʊmˈmeɪd/	_____ vanilla ice cream is my favourite.	fait(e) maison
Just water for me.	/dʒʌst ˈwɔːtə fə mi/	_____ Still water, please.	Seulement de l'eau pour moi.
Oh dear! Never mind.	/əʊ ˈdɪə ˈnevə maɪnd/	I didn't pass my exam. ~ _____	Oh zut ! Ce n'est pas grave.
porridge n	/ˈpɒrɪdʒ/	_____ is a hot breakfast cereal.	porridge
prize n	/praɪz/	The _____ in this quiz show is one million pounds.	prix
seafood n	/ˈsiːfuːd/	Can I have the _____ risotto, please?	fruits de mer
Still or sparkling?	/stɪl ɔː ˈspɑːklɪŋ/	_____ Would you like a glass or a bottle?	Plate ou pétillante, gazeuse ?
sushi n	/ˈsuːʃi/	_____ is a typical Japanese dish made with rice.	sushi
trivia n	/ˈtrɪviə/	Pat is obsessed with _____, and beat the other contestants.	connaissances de culture générale
Well done!	/ˌwel ˈdʌn/	I got all the exercises right. ~ _____	Bravo !
What would you like to drink?	/wɒt wəd ju laɪk tə ˈdrɪŋk/	_____ ~ A bottle of mineral water, please.	Que souhaitez-vous boire ?
win v	/wɪn/	How much do they ___ if they get the first answer right?	gagner
Would you like a dessert?	/wəd ju laɪk ə dɪˈzɜːt/	_____ ~ Not for me, thanks.	Souhaitez-vous un dessert ?

File 10

Vocabulary Banks

PLACES AND BUILDINGS

art gallery n	/ˈɑːt ɡaləri/	The Louvre is an _____ in Paris.	galerie d'art
bridge n	/brɪdʒ/	The Golden Gate _____ is in San Francisco.	pont
bus station n	/ˈbʌs steɪʃn/	The bus leaves the _____ at six.	gare routière
car park n	/ˈkɑː pɑːk/	I left my car in the _____.	parking
castle n	/ˈkɑːsl/	Comlongon is a 15th-century _____ in a village in Scotland.	château
chemist's/pharmacy n	/ˈkemɪsts/ˈfɑːməsi/	I need to go to the _____ to buy some medicine.	pharmacie
church n	/tʃɜːtʃ/	A _____ is a Christian building.	église
department store n	/dɪˈpɑːtmənt stɔː/	That new _____ is great.	grand magasin
hospital n	/ˈhɒspɪtl/	My father is a doctor at the local _____.	hôpital
market n	/ˈmɑːkɪt/	The _____ sells great fresh fruit.	marché
mosque n	/mɒsk/	A _____ is an Islamic building.	mosquée
museum n	/mjuˈziːəm/	The _____ is closed on Sunday.	musée
police station n	/pəˈliːs steɪʃn/	The _____ is in the town hall.	commissariat de police, gendarmerie [Suisse]
post office n	/ˈpəʊst ɒfɪs/	You can buy stamps in the _____.	poste
railway station n	/ˈreɪlweɪ steɪʃn/	I get to the _____ at six.	gare ferroviaire
river n	/ˈrɪvə/	The Coroico _____ lies far below the road.	fleuve
road n	/rəʊd/	The _____ is only about three metres wide.	route
shopping centre/mall n	/ˈʃɒpɪŋ sentə/mɔːl/	We went to a _____ to choose a dress for a party.	centre commercial
square n	/skweə/	Let's have a drink at one of those cafés in the _____.	place
street n	/striːt/	Our house is the biggest house in the _____.	rue

supermarket n	/ˈsuːpəmɑːkɪt/	I buy all my food at the _____.	supermarché
temple n	/ˈtempl/	A _____ is a Buddhist building.	temple
theatre n	/ˈθɪətə/	The Globe is a Shakespeare _____.	théâtre
town hall n	/taʊn ˈhɔːl/	The police station is in the _____.	mairie, maison communale [Belqique]

Useful words and phrases

above prep	/əˈbʌv/	They start at La Cumbre, which is 4,700 metres _____ sea level.	au-dessus
below prep	/bɪˈləʊ/	The Coroico river lies far _____ the road.	en dessous
couch n	/kaʊtʃ/	If they don't have a bed, you can sleep on their _____.	canapé
experienced adj	/ɪkˈspɪəriənst/	During the rainy season only _____ cyclists can take part.	expérimenté(e)
fewer det	/ˈfjuːə/	There are _____ buses and lorries on the old road.	moins de
fun adj	/fʌn/	A lot of people said it was ____ but I was scared.	amusant(e)
I prefer to (go to...)	/aɪ prɪˈfɜːr tə (gəʊ tə...)/	_____ the cinema than the theatre.	Je préfère aller (à/au...)
Let's (go to...)	/lets (gəʊ tə...)/	_____ the theatre.	Aller (à/au...)
mountain n	/ˈmaʊntən/	Ben Nevis is a _____ in Scotland.	montagne
narrow adj	/ˈnærəʊ/	They travel at nearly 80 km an hour down the _____ road.	étroit(e)
nearly adv	/ˈnɪəli/	They travel at _____ 80 km an hour down the narrow road.	presque
rainy adj	/ˈreɪni/	During the _____ season only experienced cyclists can take part.	pluvieux/pluvieuse
see the sights	/siː ðə ˈsaɪts/	Some hosts take their guests to _____, but others don't.	aller voir les sites touristiques
show somebody round your town/city	/ʃəʊ sʌmbədi raʊnd jɔː ˈtaʊn/ˈsɪti/	Imagine you have to _____. Where would you take them?	faire visiter la ville à quelqu'un
stay in a hotel/with a friend/for a week	/steɪ ɪn ə həʊˈtel/wɪð ə ˈfrend/fɔːr ə ˈwiːk/	I'm going to _____ in Dubai this summer.	séjourner à l'hôtel/chez un ami/pendant une semaine
the biggest adj	/ðə ˈbɪgɪst/	Kielce isn't _____ or the most beautiful town in Poland.	le/la plus grand(e)
the busiest adj	/ðə ˈbɪziɪst/	Rush hour is _____ time of day.	le/la plus fréquenté(e)
the longest adj	/ðə ˈlɒŋgɪst/	It felt like _____ car journey ever.	le/la plus long(ue)
the most beautiful adj	/ðə məʊst ˈbjuːtɪfl/	Kielce isn't the biggest or _____ town in Poland.	le/la plus beau/belle
the most dangerous adj	/ðə məʊst ˈdeɪndʒərəs/	What's _____ area to walk in at night?	le/la plus dangereux/dangereuse
the most exciting adj	/ðə məʊst ɪkˈsaɪtɪŋ/	Mountain bikers come to have _____ ride of their lives.	le/la plus excitant(e)
the most expensive adj	/ðə məʊst ɪkˈspensɪv/	What's _____ present you've ever bought?	le/la plus cher/chère
the most popular adj	/ðə məʊst ˈpɒpjələ/	What's _____ area to go to at night?	le/la plus populaire
the oldest adj	/ðə ˈəʊldɪst/	What's _____ building in your town?	le/la plus vieux/vielle
the smallest adj	/ðə ˈsmɔːlɪst/	This is _____ shop in town.	le/la plus petit(e)
the widest adj	/ðə ˈwaɪdɪst/	Avenida 9 de Julio in Buenos Aires is _____ street in the world.	le/la plus large
Why don't we (go to...)?	/ˈwaɪ dəʊnt wi (gəʊ tə...)/	_____ the shopping mall?	Pourquoi ne pas (aller à/au...) ?

More words in File 10

basket n	/ˈbɑːskɪt/	Your shopping _____ is full of junk food.	panier
be lucky	/biː ˈlʌki/	I want to _____.	avoir de la chance
become famous	/bɪkʌm ˈfeɪməs/	Do you think you're going to _____?	devenir célèbre
compared with	/kəmˈpeəd wɪð/	My house is small _____ other houses in the area.	comparé(e) à

crisis n	/ˈkraɪsɪs/	During a _____, e.g. divorce or losing a job, people eat more junk food.	crise
fall in love	/fɔːl ɪn ˈlʌv/	You are going to _____.	tomber amoureux
get a lot of money	/get ə lɒt ɒv ˈmʌni/	You are going to _____.	gagner beaucoup d'argent
get a new job	/get ə njuː ˈdʒɒb/	I want to _____.	trouver un nouvel emploi
get married	/get ˈmærid/	I'm going to _____.	se marier
government n	/ˈgʌvənmənt/	The _____ says people in the UK need to have a healthier diet.	gouvernement
have a surprise	/hæv ə səˈpraɪz/	I hope I'm going to _____.	avoir une surprise
however conj	/haʊˈevə/	He felt ill. He went to work, _____, and tried to work hard.	cependant
junk food n	/ˈdʒʌŋk fuːd/	Do you ever buy _____, e.g. frozen pizzas, crisps, and cakes?	alimentation malsaine
meet somebody new	/miːt sʌmbədi ˈnjuː/	You are going to _____.	faire une nouvelle rencontre
moon n	/muːn/	Look at the _____!	lune
move house	/muːv ˈhaʊs/	I'm going to _____.	déménager
ready-made meal n	/ˈredi ˌmeɪd ˈmiːl/	I'm too tired to cook. I'll have a _____.	plat préparé
soon adv	/suːn/	And very _____ you're going to get married.	bientôt
spoon n	/spuːn/	Can you pass me a _____?	cuillère
survey n	/ˈsɜːveɪ/	A _____ showed that many people have unhealthy eating habits.	sondage

File 11

Useful words and phrases

attachment n	/əˈtætʃmənt/	I'm sending an _____ with this email.	pièce jointe
beautifully adv	/ˈbjuːtɪfli/	My niece plays the piano _____.	merveilleusement
become v	/bɪˈkʌm/	I wish my brother hadn't _____ a Goth.	devenir
bite v	/baɪt/	I _____ my nails when I'm nervous.	se ronger (les ongles)
carefully adv	/ˈkeəfəli/	He wrote down the phone number _____.	soigneusement
casually adv	/ˈkæʒuəli/	She dresses _____ at the weekends.	de manière décontractée
choose v	/tʃuːz/	_____ five things you really like and make a recipe using them.	choisir
climb v	/klaɪm/	I'd like to _____ a mountain somewhere beautiful next year.	gravir, grimper [Suisse]
download v	/ˌdaʊnˈləʊd/	Be careful when you _____ new programs.	télécharger
fashionably adv	/ˈfæʃnəbli/	He dresses _____.	à la mode
go on a safari	/gəʊ ɒn ə səˈfɑːri/	Would you like to _____?	partir en safari
incredibly slowly adv	/ɪnkredəbli ˈsləʊli/	People in this city speak _____.	incroyablement lentement
learn v	/lɜːn/	I want to _____ to cook before I leave home.	apprendre
log in phr v	/lɒg ˈɪn/	You need to _____ before you can use the internet.	se connecter
online adj	/ˌɒnˈlaɪn/	How often do you go _____?	en ligne
perfectly adv	/ˈpɜːfɪktli/	My sister speaks Spanish _____.	parfaitement
politely adv	/pəˈlaɪtli/	You must speak _____ when working with customers.	poliment
quite dangerously adv	/kwaɪt ˈdeɪndʒərəsli/	I think people drive _____ in my country.	assez dangereusement
search for v	/ˈsɜːtʃ fɔː/	You should _____ a job on the internet.	rechercher
social network n	/ˈsəʊʃl ˈnetwɜːk/	Have you ever used a _____?	réseau social

upload v	/ˌʌpˈləʊd/	How do I _____ the program?	télécharger
wifi n	/ˈwaɪ faɪ/	Is there ___ in this hotel?	wifi, wi-fi

More words in File 11

Can I pay by credit card?	/kən aɪ peɪ baɪ ˈkredɪt kɑːd/	_____ I don't have any cash.	Puis-je payer par carte bancaire ?
coach n	/kəʊtʃ/	We use a _____ to take the children on school days out.	autocar, bus [Suisse]
Have a good journey.	/həv ə gʊd ˈdʒɜːni/	_____ and see you next month.	Bon voyage.
How much is it?	/haʊ ˈmʌtʃ ɪz ɪt/	_____ to go from London to Manchester?	Combien ça coûte ?
I can't believe it!	/aɪ kɑːnt bɪˈliːv ɪt/	_____ I won the competition!	Je n'arrive pas à y croire.
See you in [New York].	/siː juː ɪn njuː ˈjɔːk/	_____ New York in September.	On se voit à [New York]
Single or return?	/ˈsɪŋgl ɔː rɪˈtɜːn/	_____ ~ Single, please.	Aller simple ou aller-retour ?
Standard or first class?	/ˈstændəd ɔː fɜːst ˈklɑːs/	_____ ~ Standard, please.	Classe économique ou première classe ?
tram n	/træm/	I like to travel by ____ when I am in Germany.	tramway

File 12

Useful words and phrases

dangerously adv	/ˈdeɪndʒərəsli/	My mum drives really _____.	dangereusement
decide v	/dɪˈsaɪd/	I can't _____ what subject to study at university.	décider
ever adv	/ˈevə/	Have you ____ been on TV?	déjà
formal adj	/ˈfɔːml/	You need to wear _____ clothes for the dinner party.	habillé(e)
healthcare n	/ˈhelθkeə/	_____ in the UK is free.	soins médicaux
healthily adv	/ˈhelθɪli/	Frank eats very _____.	sainement
informal adj	/ɪnˈfɔːml/	Emails are often more _____ than letters.	informel/informelle
insurance n	/ɪnˈʃʊərəns/	You need to have health _____ in the US.	assurance
on the other hand	/ɒn ðə ˈʌðə hænd/	British people are quite reserved, but _____ it is harder to make friends in the US than in the UK.	d'un autre côté
perhaps adv	/pəˈhæps/	_____ the living room is my favourite room in the house.	peut-être
pessimistic adj	/ˌpesɪˈmɪstɪk/	I find British people quite _____.	pessimiste
portion n	/ˈpɔːʃn/	I'm not hungry, so I'll just have a small _____.	portion
professional adj	/prəˈfeʃənl/	It's my dream to become a _____ actor.	professionnel
promise v	/ˈprɒmɪs/	_____ that you'll send me a postcard from your holiday.	promettre
queue n	/kjuː/	I talk to everyone – even people next to me in the _____.	file d'attente
real adj	/rɪəl/	____ friends are hard to find.	vrai(e)
reserved adj	/rɪˈzɜːvd/	Some people say that British people are too _____.	réservé(e)
the cost of living n	/ðə kɒst əv ˈlɪvɪŋ/	_____ is really high in London.	le coût de la vie
traditional adj	/trəˈdɪʃənl/	My favourite kind of music is _____ American jazz.	traditionnel/traditionelle
unhealthily adv	/ʌnˈhelθɪli/	Julia eats really _____.	de manière malsaine
website n	/ˈwebsaɪt/	What's your favourite _____?	site Web
wide variety n	/waɪd vəˈraɪəti/	In the UK you can buy a _____ of food.	grande variété
worst adj	/wɜːst/	The _____ thing was living away from home for a year or more.	pire